HYDROPONICS

AND

GREENHOUSE

GARDENING

3 IN 1 GARDENING BOOK TO GROW VEGETABLES,
HERBS AND FRUIT ALL-YEAR-ROUND

RICHARD BRAY

Published by *Monkey Publishing*

Edited by *Lily Marlene Booth*

Cover Design by *Diogo Lando*

Cover images: *Chatree.l, Rawpixel/Shutterstock.com*

Jira Saki/Stocksy United

Printed by *Amazon*

1st Edition, published in 2019

© 2019 by Monkey Publishing

Lerchenstrasse 111

22767 Hamburg

Germany

ISBN: 9781708119683

MONKEY
PUBLISHING

OUR HAND-PICKED
BOOK SELECTION FOR YOU.

LEARN
SOMETHING NEW
EVERYDAY.

YOUR FREE BONUS

As a small token of thanks for buying this book, I am offering a free bonus gift to my readers. Hydroponics is a new and innovative way of growing plants, but that doesn't mean it's difficult. As with anything new, there will be a learning curve at the beginning. To accelerate your learning, the free bonus offers additional tips for successful hydroponic gardening practices.

In this bonus package, you will learn:

- How to set and control the climate for your plants

- 9 tips on how to regulate water temperature easily

- How to keep the oxygen and nutritional levels well balanced

- Simple ways to keep your roots healthy and thriving

- A 15- step formula to raise your seeds successfully

You can download the free gift here:
https://hydroponicsbundle.gr8.com/

TABLE OF CONTENTS – ALL BOOKS

Book 1

Book 2

Book 3

HYDRO PONICS

HOW TO PICK THE BEST HYDROPONIC SYSTEM AND CROPS FOR HOMEGROWN FOOD YEAR-ROUND

RICHARD BRAY

TABLE OF CONTENTS

CHAPTER 1: THE BASICS OF HYDROPONICS

Chatree.l/Shutterstock.com

You don't need to be a farmer to begin your own hydroponic garden. Nor do you need acres of land. All you need is a willingness to learn.

Hydroponics has been around for at least 500 years. The first book on the subject was published by Francis Bacon in the 17th century. Since then, there have been numerous innovations in the field, but the basics remain the same. This method of farming can be used both indoors and outside. All you need is a basic understanding of how to set up your hydroponics growing system(s), and you're off!

What you are about to create with the help of this hydroponic guide is a method of growing vegetables, herbs and fruit at home without the use of soil. The roots will instead rely on a nutritionally enriched liquid. They are nourished in water, supplemented with liquid nutrients. You can use mediums, such as perlite and vermiculite, or even rockwool and clay pellets, but more on that later.

There are many ways to create a hydroponic system. You can either buy a kit or you can assemble a system from scratch with your own equipment. Ready-made kits are a great option if you want to save time and effort and jump straight into the growing process. They also won't require too much explanation, as the process is fairly simple once you begin. So, while we'll cover ready-made kits, much of the book will be devoted to DIY hydroponics. DIY hydroponics is easier and more rewarding than you might expect, and this book will give you all you need to know to begin your hydroponic journey.

Anton Teplyakov/Shutterstock.com

There are various ways of running your hydroponic garden. In this book, I will explain each method to help you decide which one works best for your personal situation. Then, you will be ready to buy a kit, or put together a system using your own equipment, according to the method you choose. To do so, you need to consider the following:

- **What is the size of the space for your hydroponics setup?**

If you are new to hydroponic farming, then it is better to start small.

- **Is it indoors or outside?**

If you are fortunate enough to have a reasonably sized yard, then you should consider setting up a greenhouse system. Hydroponics can be set up outside but might be more prone to pests or the vagaries of the weather. If you have a spare indoor room, you will need to consider the light source.

- **Cost?**

There are some pieces of equipment you will need, but you can limit the cost if you start small.

- **What type of plants do you wish to grow?**

You can grow just about any plant using hydroponic growing, such as vegetables, fruits, salads, herbs and even flowers.

- **What time do you have available for maintenance?**

If you are a novice, it is better to grow fast-growing plants. There are plenty to choose from, such as lettuce, parsley, tomatoes or strawberries. None of these are particularly time consuming to grow. This way you learn at a steady pace and can change your system, or plants, as you become more experienced. If you enjoy it, then you can move on to more complex plants.

PROS/CONS OF HYDROPONIC GARDENING

One of the most outstanding features of growing using this method is that plants use much less water than they would if grown as crops in the ground. Hydroponic farming uses only 10% of the water that traditional ground crops use. Now that's a figure worth considering.

Could this be the future of farming in countries where water is a scarce resource? Already it is growing more popular. So, let's look at the positive features of a hydroponic garden, or farming system:

PROS

No Soil, Less Land

No soil is needed whatsoever. Your plants will grow in a water-based system. Liquid nutrients will help them grow to maturity. The vast acres of land now used for farming can be used for other needs such as housing and forestry. It also means that more vegetation can be grown in smaller plots.

Less Water

You can grow plants anywhere, at any time of the year, regardless of climate. The system you choose will only use a set amount of water according to the size of your farming system. With the aid of simple equipment, the plant roots sit in the water. This is unlike field crops whereby the water either soaks off into the ground or dries up with the heat of the sun. The water in your system can be re-used time and time again, so you are recycling it. No irrigation of the land is needed, resulting in lower costs for the farmer.

Fewer Nutrients, Less Fertilizer

Nutrients are fed to the plants in a controlled environment instead of running off and soaking into the ground, polluting land and rivers. Imagine a farming world without the need for spraying fertilizer all over the land.

More Crops, Fewer Enemies

The indoor systems, such as inside your home or in a greenhouse, have many advantages. There is no loss of crops due to bad weather. Wild animals cannot eat the plants as they can with field crops. With no soil, there will also be fewer pests and diseases to contend with.

The outdoor systems still work efficiently but if your hydroponic garden is not protected, then it could still be prone to problems from pests and the weather.

Healthier Crops

Crops grown by the hydroponic method enjoy 100% of the nutrients fed to them. None will soak into the ground or be blown away by the wind. The result of this is that they produce up to 30% more foliage than soil grown plants and grow 25% faster. It is all down to the well-balanced nutrients the roots receive from the water.

Fewer Chemicals Needed

With fewer parasitic bugs, fewer insecticides and herbicides are needed. The result is healthier food for human consumption.

Weather Resistant

Hydroponic crops grown indoors are not weather dependent. They can be grown all year round, regardless of the climate or temperature. Crops are more protected if grown indoors or in greenhouses.

Less Labor

There will be no labor-intensive weeding necessary, either chemically, or by hand. This lowers the need for maintenance. There will be the initial seeding, feeding, and harvesting processes, but these can be achieved with much less labor than the traditional methods of growing crops.

Can be Grown Anywhere, Geographically

This method does not rely on available land. The farm could be set up near to the market where the crops will be sold. It's a great way of cutting down on transport costs and pollution. It can even be mobile, if necessary, and set up wherever and whenever needed.

A Method to Suit all Budgets

There are many methods of growing crops using a hydroponic system. It can be a small-scale affair in your backyard or indoors in a spare room. But, it can also be done on an industrial scale. Large volumes of produce with thousands of plants for a nation of people can be achieved using hydroponic farming.

Cons

Plants are dependent on humans. Nature has little to do with this type of farming. The plants are relying on human attention for everything, from water to food, to light and humidity. Once the garden is up and running, it can go into automation for the most part. Though as with all farming, someone must regulate it. If it is not done correctly, whole crops can be lost.

Requires some Expertise

This is not a traditional method of growing plants. A certain amount of knowledge on the various systems is required. Done incorrectly, the whole crop of plants could perish.

Safety

Everyone is aware that water and electricity are a dangerous combination. Hydroponic plants need both water and electricity to manage the entire system. If mistakes happen, it could cause a life-threatening situation.

Electric Failure

What would happen if the electricity supply was down for any amount of time? This must be considered from the onset. If such a thing were to occur, without emergency provision, the whole crop could die in hours.

Initial Outlay for Large Farms

There is a need to buy equipment when you first set up your hydroponic system. That can be costly if farming on a large scale. Once established, the running costs will be electricity, water, and nutrients. Plus a small labor force if it is a large farm.

Fast Spreading Diseases

The chances of soil disease are nil, so pests and diseases are fewer. However, if your system gets a water-based disease, this will spread rapidly to any plants on the same system. A means of measuring the water for such bacteria needs to be put in place to avoid this happening. Otherwise, you could lose your entire crop to disease.

Chapter 2: Overview Of The Different Hydroponic Systems

Now that we know why hydroponic is a good alternative to soil gardening, it is time to look at the different systems. In this chapter, we will look at six different ways of growing crops hydroponically. Once armed with this knowledge, it will allow you to assess which system is best for your own personal situation.

Of course, you may want to run more than one system, depending on space available, and the type of plants you wish to grow. First though, let's go over the growing techniques.

Drip System

The Drip System is one of the most popular hydroponic systems. It is employed world-wide both for personal and commercial use.

- Basically, water and nutrients are slow-dripped into the growing tray which houses the plant's roots.

- This system is ideal for plants with larger roots and for growing in hotter climates where water is sparse.

- As with most hydroponic systems, the drip system requires two tanks. One tank is the growing tray which houses the plant roots in a suitable growing medium. Beneath this is the reservoir tank, which stores water and nutrients and contains the pumps.

- There are two pumps in this system. One delivers nutrient-rich water to the growing tray from the main reservoir. This can be controlled by a timer switch. The second pump aerates the water in the main reservoir with the aid of an air stone.

- With the help of the air pump, air stones deliver to the tank many small bubbles that are filled with oxygen. While an air pump and tube can function without the use of an air stone at the end of the line, growers prefer air stones, which help diffuse the oxygen better than the larger tube can without it.

- The drip line is the tube which supplies nutrient-rich water to the plants. Liquid drips out of the emitters, which control the amount of water each plant receives. The water lands on the growing media and drains down to feed the roots. Each plant needs its own drip line.

- Gravity drains any excess liquid into the reservoir where it can be recycled.

It is important to keep the growing medium damp. It should not be allowed to become either soaked through or completely dry.

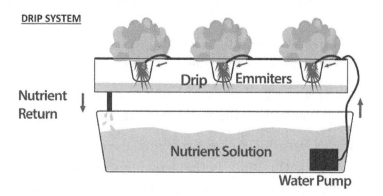

The Drip Method can perform in one of two ways. It can be either recirculating/recovery or non-recirculating/non-recovery. The names of the systems are self-explanatory. They refer to whether or not the water is recycled.

- *Recirculating/recovery* systems are often used by home growers to keep costs down. The nutrient-rich water is not always used up by the plants. Rather than draining away, it returns to the reservoir tank via an overflow pipe. With this method, any water that collects in the bottom of the growing tray is recirculated through the system. The grower needs to check the pH levels of this system periodically. This is because nutrients will tend to become watered down in the recovery process. Also, the grower will need to top up the reservoir tank with nutritional solution from time to time.

- *Non-recirculating/non-recovery* is more popular when using the Drip System on a larger scale. With this method, excess water runs off as waste. It requires an extra piece of equipment called a Cycle Timer. This will add fresh nutrients into the main reservoir tank at timed intervals. Every now and then the growing media will need flushing with fresh water to prevent mineral build-up and algae growth.

EBB AND FLOW

- Also known as the Flood and Drain System.

- Popular with home growers.

- The medium that contains the roots is flooded at timed intervals. A flow of nutrient-enriched water is provided by a pump from the main reservoir, which again, sits below the grow tray. Water then returns to the main reservoir through a gravity-powered overflow pipe.

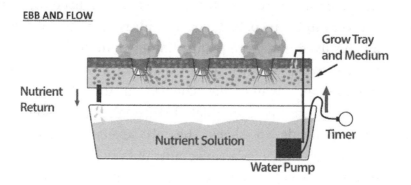

EBB AND FLOW

Grow Tray and Medium

Nutrient Return

Nutrient Solution

Timer

Water Pump

Here are some of the variations of the Ebb and Flow method:

- Tray Container

In this method, plants sit on a layer of growing medium in a large tray. Nutrient-enriched water is pumped through a tube from the bottom reservoir into the growing tray. When the water reaches a certain level, the overflow returns to the reservoir below. One disadvantage of this system is that it can be difficult to remove individual plants as the roots can become entwined.

- Separate Containers

Plants sit in separate pots, each containing a growing medium. The pots are placed in a large tray which fills with water. The rest of the procedure is the same as the tray method, with water draining back down to the reservoir. One advantage of this system is that individual plants can be removed easily because they are in separate pots.

- Surge

The main difference between the surge method and other variations of Ebb and Flow is that the reservoir tank does not need to be below the growing tray. There are still two tanks: the reservoir and the surge tank. The surge tank, which is at the same level as the growing pots, feeds the nutrient-enriched water via a pump. The growing pots are connected to the surge tank via pipes that sit below the water line.

The principle is that the water in the surge tank is at the same level as it is in the growing pots. When the water in the surge tank reaches a certain level, a pump is activated. This returns the water to the main tank. As the water in the surge tank drops, so does the water in the growing pots. This system is more expensive to construct as there are more parts required.

The size of your water pump depends on the design of your hydroponic system. It is advisable to get a bigger pump than you actually think you'll need, because you can always reduce the water flow but not vice versa. You can use simple submersible fountain and pond pumps for your hydroponic system.

NUTRIENT FILM TECHNIQUE

- Ideal for small, quick-growing plants.

- The reservoir tank sits underneath the growing compartments and contains nutrient-enriched water. This water is pumped to separate grow channels.

- The growing compartments are usually gullies or tubes that allow the water to flow through. Plants sit in a basket on the tray with their roots suspended through a hole. This method allows the roots to access the nutritional flow of water in the bottom of the gully.

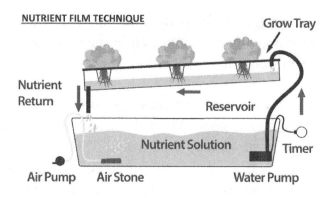

NUTRIENT FILM TECHNIQUE

- Nutrient-enriched water is pumped up through a tube. It enters one end of a growing channel which sits on an angle.

- Water flows down the slope and returns through a waste pipe situated at the other end of the gullies. The roots act like a wick and soak up the liquid.

- This method requires accurate measurement of flow rate and a correct slant angle in order to be effective.

- The flow is constant, so the pump must be active at all times.

- Roots are more exposed in this system. Because of this, it is important to monitor humidity and temperature levels. If you don't, the roots could dry out or become waterlogged, which could result in the loss of the entire crop.

- You need to watch out for roots clogging the system and blocking the water flow.

WATER CULTURE

- Popular for commercial farming as it is an inexpensive method for large-scale usage. It is equally as popular with the smaller homesteaders because there are low initial setup costs and it can be as small or large as the available space.

- Only uses one tank. The main tank houses both the nutritional water and the plants. Some growers use interconnected growing tanks and circulate the water between them. However, this requires a pump.

- Plants sit with their roots suspended in the water via hanging baskets. Alternately, holes can be cut into the lid of the reservoir tank. The plant sits in the lid with its roots suspended in the water through the holes.

- No water pump is required because plants sit in the nutritional water continuously.

- You'll need to top up the tank with water and nutrients well as they are used up by the plants.

WATER CULTURE

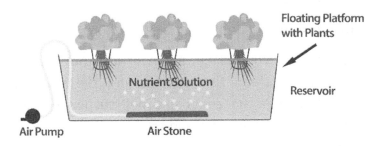

- A system of aeration is needed to ensure the plants receive the necessary oxygen.

Here are some options you have for oxygenating the water:

- Air Pump

Pumps the oxygen into an air stone that sits on the bottom of the tank. Air bubbles rise into the water for the roots.

- Waterfall

Water cascades into the tank at force, agitating and aerating the water in the reservoir.

- Recirculating Water

Similar to the Ebb and Flow System. The water never completely drains out and the roots are always submerged. Water is pumped into the growing pots, ensuring the plants receive sufficient oxygen to thrive. Once the water reaches a certain level, it is returned to the reservoir via an overflow.

AEROPONICS

- Would you believe that this is fast becoming popular in modern restaurants? It allows them to grow their own products and display them in growing towers. Aeroponics is known as vertical farming and is one of the leading hydroponic systems in commercial industries. It's a great method for any indoor gardener.

- Only one tank is required for Aeroponic systems.

- Roots hang down through holes in the lid of the tank. The difference between this system and the water culture method is that the roots are not suspended in water. Instead, they remain exposed to the air. This makes for an oxygen rich atmosphere.

- The plants do not need any growing medium.

- The tank has nutrients and water at the bottom and a pump for water delivery.

- The roots are sprayed by water and nutrients in short bursts from a sprinkler underneath. This requires that the sprinkling system be set up inside the tank.

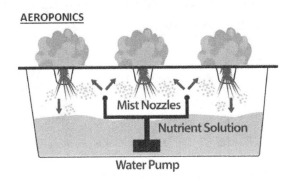

AEROPONICS

Mist Nozzles

Nutrient Solution

Water Pump

- The growing tank is the most important element of this system. When set up correctly, it retains humidity and allows for a constant flow of fresh oxygen.

- The tank should be airtight so pests cannot get inside. This will protect the exposed roots.

- If the pump stops for any reason, the roots can dry up quickly and the entire crop may be lost.

- This spray method can be set up in different ways. Each system will alter the size of the droplets in the sprinkling: High Pressure, Low Pressure and Foggers. The higher the pressure, the larger the droplets. The Fogger has the smallest droplets and provides water in the form of a mist.

WICK IRRIGATION

- This is the simplest method. It is also the most cost-effective means of growing plants hydroponically.

- Requires no use of pump or electricity.

- Only one tank is needed. The plant containers sit above the reservoir that contains the nutrients and water. A wick(s) hangs down and drops into the water solution. It soaks up the nutritional water, which in turn dampens the plant medium, to feed the roots.

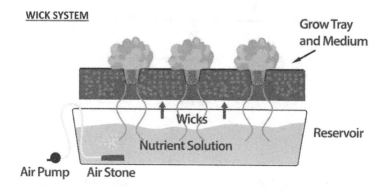

- The system can be as simple as one plant pot that sits above the reservoir. Its wick hangs down and enters through a hole. Larger systems could include several plants in a tray with multiple wicks dangling into the solution.

- The growing medium will need flushing periodically to stop algae or mineral build up.

CHAPTER 3: CHOOSE THE RIGHT HYDROPONIC SYSTEM FOR YOU

B ear in mind, that for many new hydroponic gardeners, it may be a case of trial and error for the first year. It can take time to discover exactly what fits your needs. There may be failures along the way, however I encourage you to persevere. It will be well worth all the effort because your plants will be bountiful once you succeed.

Bluedog studios/Shutterstock.com

CONSIDERING PERSONAL CIRCUMSTANCES

We have arrived at the point of decision making. Here I want you to look closer at your own situation and think about how you can decide which hydroponic system will best suit your own lifestyle. I will break this section up with each system, considering our list of:

- Space
- Budget
- Experience
- Time

SPACE

At the beginning of the book, I wrote about indoor or outdoor hydroponic gardening.

If you choose to set up outdoors, without any surrounding protection, your plants will be prone to pest attacks.

This can be reduced somewhat if you have a greenhouse in which to grow your crops. A traditional glass house or a plastic tent tunnel works fine. If you grow your crops indoors, then your plants will be much less prone to pests. However, your space may be more limited indoors.

If you are considering growing plants that are not the norm for your climate, then you will either need a greenhouse or to grow indoors.

If you wish to grow out of season plants, then they will need special care with their environment.

In either circumstance, you will need to consider providing artificial lighting, heating and control the humidity. These cannot be set up in the open and must be under a protective covering, such as a greenhouse, or alternatively, indoors.

BUDGET

The complexity of the system you have is also dependent on your available funds. You can begin and should begin, with a small, simple system, such as Water Culture. As you advance, that's when you will begin to spend more.

You could put all your equipment together yourself by purchasing each part separately. The only trouble you may find is that you might buy the wrong pieces and end up spending more than you intended.

There are ready-made kits available for each system. They will contain the exact materials you will need for that particular hydroponic system. At least that way, you will only be buying the necessary equipment for your project. Although kits tend to be more expensive than the DIY option, in the long run, this could save you money.

If you are good at DIY, then you may be able to improvise containers and piping. Or even buy second-hand bits and pieces, such as a pond pump. You must clean and disinfect everything thoroughly before use.

EXPERIENCE

Whether you wish to grow specialty plants, or the easier ones, such as lettuces and herbs, the key to growth is always:

- Humidity
- Water Temperature
- pH levels
- Nutritional strengths

Get these right, and you should have yourself a bountiful crop.

From the initial seeding to caring for the roots, from lighting and all the different ways of measuring levels, it all comes down to practice. If you are already a keen gardener, then you will already have much of the knowledge needed for caring for plants. The experience of hydroponic gardening will come later, with time and practice. You must consider all these factors though, before deciding which system is best for you.

TIME

How much time you spend on your self-sufficient garden is up to you. Choose a method that you know will work around your present timetable and lifestyle. The busier you are, then the smaller your system should be. It stands to reason that the fewer plants you have, the less time is needed. As with any garden, you will need to care for your plants. Measuring of varying levels will need to be done. Flushing of systems should be undertaken regularly.

To help you choose, I have gone through each hydroponic method to give you an idea of all these factors: Space, Budget, Experience and Time. I hope this will help you choose which hydroponic system is the right one for you.

WHICH SYSTEM WORKS BEST FOR YOU?

DRIP SYSTEM

- **Space**

A basic drip system is achievable for any beginner. It will take up a little more room because there are two large containers. Ideally, the system could sit on a table.

- **Budget**

There is more equipment to buy using this method. You will need at least one circulating pump, a timer, and tubing. You will also want a drip manifold. If the budget is tight, you can make small holes in the tubing instead. This system requires a growing medium.

It can be less expensive to run than the Water Culture, or Ebb and Flow, systems. This is because it makes more efficient use of the nutrients, therefore using less of them. This may not make much difference to a smaller garden. To benefit from this, you would need at least 10+ plants in the system.

- **Experience**

It is a little complicated to set up. This method is more sophisticated than Water Culture, which can be done in a single bucket. It is also more complex to set up than the Ebb and Flow method. If you are a beginner, it might be better to buy a ready-made kit that has all the right components in one place.

Be aware that tubing can become blocked with the excess minerals from the nutrient liquid. Be vigilant of this because your crop could soon dry up and die from not receiving any water.

A higher skill level is needed with this system. You need a basic understanding of balancing the concentration of nutrients. You also need a good knowledge of how often the pump should be on and off. Get these wrong and your plants will suffer. If it is not enough, then the roots could be stunted, or even worse, dry out. If it is too much, the roots could rot or grow a fungus.

This system relies on electrical power. Make sure you check it periodically and know what to do if it goes off.

- **Time**

There are a few maintenance tasks that will require attention. The flow of nutrients should always be well balanced. Check the pipes often so they don't get blocked. Should the electricity cut off, the whole system will come to a stop. It is vital you check it often because you can lose your entire crop.

Each of these issues is very important to the success of your garden. Failure on any of these points and your crop may die.

EBB AND FLOW

- **Space**

Very similar in space requirements to the Drip System. The growing tray should be sitting on a table with the reservoir container underneath so it can make full use of gravity. This system works well indoors.

- **Budget**

To set this system up, you will need to buy some basic equipment, such as a pump, tubing, timer and medium.

- **Experience**

It is easy to maintain, once you get the hang of it. However, it can be a little complicated to set up. If DIY is not your thing, then there are ready-made kits to buy containing everything you need.

Measuring temperature and pH levels is not quite so important with this method. However you should still measure these levels, just not as often.

- **Time**

Nutrient water in the reservoir will need changing every 7-10 days. Also, after a harvest, the system will need a thorough clean with hydrogen peroxide. It is best to check pH levels daily so you can adjust them if needed. You need to check on a regular basis that the pump is working and the tubing has not become blocked.

NUTRIENT FILM TECHNIQUE

- **Space**

The grow tray is usually a gulley or channel, so it can be lengthy. You also need space for a reservoir tank that holds the nutrient-enriched water. Again, it is better if the grow tray is situated on top and the reservoir below. Like many hydroponic systems, if it is kept small, it can be set up inside.

- **Budget**

As it is a constant flow system, you will need a pump, but a timer is not necessary. It is an inexpensive way to start your hydroponic growing, however it is also a little complicated, so do bear this in mind. No medium is required. The plants are held in baskets, in a lid with holes, so the roots hang down and reach the channel of water. To ensure the reservoir water is well aerated, an air stone fed by an air circulating pump is a good option.

- **Experience**

Setting up can be tricky. The grow channels need to be at an angle so the water runs down from one end to the other. If the angle is wrong, then the plants could flood or dry out. You will need to know how to measure pH and temperature levels because these need checking every day.

- **Time**

NFT is easy to maintain with little work required to keep it working well. The biggest job is replacing the nutrient-enriched water. This needs to be done every two weeks to ensure the plants are correctly fed. After harvesting, your system will need a thorough clean out. Otherwise, harmful bacteria can build up in the growing channel and reservoir. Suspended roots can grow too long and restrict the flow of water. If this is the case, then you can trim them without harming the plants. It is important to keep the water temperatures cool, at around 68F/20C.

WATER CULTURE

- **Space**

You could start with as little as the space required for a 5-gallon bucket. Everything that you need can be comfortably confined to one container. It can become more elaborate if you wish to extend the system later. One bucket, nutrient water, and a lid with holes in it are all you need to get started on this hydroponic system. Unless you grow individual plants in pots, with the roots suspended in the nutritional water, then you don't even need a growing medium.

- **Budget**

This can be the least expensive system to set up.

It can run without a medium by hanging your plants through a hole cut in a lid. It might be better to use small baskets for the roots so the plants have some means of support.

You will need to buy medium if you choose to use plant pots for each plant.

Unless you are running a larger system, you do not need a water pump.

If you start small with the one container, you can grow 1-4 plants in the same system. This is what I recommend for the beginner. Start small, then as you gain experience, expand your system.

- **Experience**

Water Culture is one of the simplest growing systems. This means that it is easy to set up, even with a limited knowledge. Plants are fast growing in this system because their roots are in the nutritional liquid all the time. There is no need to worry about researching and choosing the right medium, as it does not need any if you wish to keep it simple.

The main things to watch out for are:

- Ensure the water temperature stays at a specific level, around 68F/20C, to maintain the oxygen levels and inhibit the growth of harmful bacteria. Keep the container in the shade and out of direct sunlight if you can. Paint the container white as this helps reflect the heat.

- You will also need to keep your eye on the pH levels of the water.

- You will need to change the nutrient water every 10 days or so. This is essential for keeping the nutrients at a prime level and preventing the buildup of harmful chemicals.

Start with only one or two plants. As you gain confidence, add to the system.

You could add another bucket and introduce a recirculating garden, however, this needs a pump. The water pumps from one bucket to the next so all the buckets are not running on an individual system.

- **Time**

It is simple to set up and can probably be achieved in half a day, depending on the size of your system.

Other than periodically checking the temperature and pH levels, the only time-consuming task will be changing the water. Each bucket must be given fresh water and nutrients.

You can cut down the time spent on this task by using a pump and the recirculating method. Basically, it means the water is pumped from one bucket to the next so all the buckets are not run individually but are using the same water. This way, when you do have to change the water, you only need to concentrate on the main bucket's solution mixture. You will still need to drain the whole system but the other buckets will soon fill up from your main bucket flow.

AEROPONICS

- **Space**

This system is not ideal for a beginner as there are few "small" Aeroponic systems. You do need lots of space to make this method worthwhile. Technically, you could have a small garden in a large tub with about six plants.

- **Budget**

This is the most expensive system to set up. You are going to need the essentials, such as filters, tubes, and pumps. You MUST also use high-quality nutrients, as low-quality ones have more salt residue and are more likely to block the sprayers.

- **Experience**

Aeroponic systems are the most difficult for a beginner. However, it is probably the system that will yield the biggest harvest.

If you do things wrong, you WILL lose your entire crop.

- **Time**

High maintenance or your crop will die.

Blockages

You'll need to conduct regular checks to ensure that the sprayers do not clog up with minerals from the nutritional liquid. If unattended, the roots will dry up and the plants will die.

Temperature

Regular temperature checks are also required, the water should be at around 64F/18C.

Humidity

The humidity levels also need constant checking and the levels can vary: i.e. vegetable or fruit stage should read 60-70%; flowering stage 30-40%. If it is too high, it will cause algae or rot, and too low will stunt growth or cause the roots to dry up. This method does have a speedy harvest cycle, so if run correctly, then the plants will grow fast.

WICK IRRIGATION

- **Space**

Ideal if you have limited space, particularly if your hydroponic garden is to be indoors. Similar in size to the Water Culture System and crops can be grown in just one bucket.

- **Budget**

A basic Wick System is one of the cheapest hydroponic methods you can use. However, it does need a growing medium and a suitable fabric to use as the wick. For this system, you will need an absorbent growing medium, such as clay, perlite or coir. Plus, you still need to buy the nutrients.

The system would benefit from an aeration pump and air-stone. If the water is still, nutrients can sink to the bottom of the feeding reservoir.

- **Experience**

Although a seemingly simple arrangement, the Wick System is not without its problems. It is easy to set up and get started. It is not very good for larger plants that need lots of water and nutrients. A novice should begin with smaller, quick-growing plants. If you are a beginner, stick to herbs or lettuces, because this system will be ideal for such crops.

The wick is important and you must use a material that will soak up liquid efficiently. Rope, fabric and felt are useful for this purpose. It may be a case of experimentation, trial, and error. If wicks do not work correctly, then the roots will dry up and the plants will die.

- **Time**

As the wick and medium can become soaked in salt minerals, this system does need regular maintenance. Plants will only soak up the nutrients they need leaving behind all those they don't want. The minerals remain in the wick and medium and can build up. To counteract this, you will need to flush the medium with fresh, clear water periodically. Plus, you will also need to top up the nutritional water reservoir.

If you don't use an air pump to create movement in the still water, you will need to stir up the reservoir water. Do this at least a couple of times a day.

CHAPTER 4: MEDIUMS, NUTRIENTS AND LIGHTING FOR THE HYDROPONIC GARDEN

Now that you have an overview of the different hydroponic systems, it is time to look at the growing mediums and nutrients needed to enable a bountiful harvest.

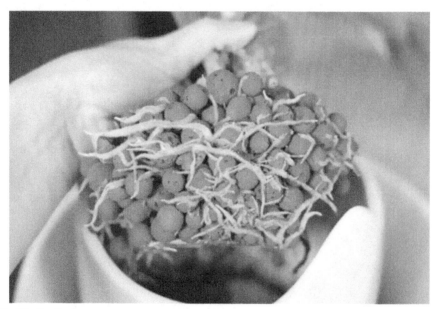

Firn/Shutterstock.com

BEST GROWING MEDIUMS FOR EACH SYSTEM

First, consider which type of medium you want to grow your plants in. Many growers combine mediums to gain all the advantages of each one.

When we talk about mediums, we are referring to the contents of the growing tray or pot that the plant's roots stand in.

Types of Mediums

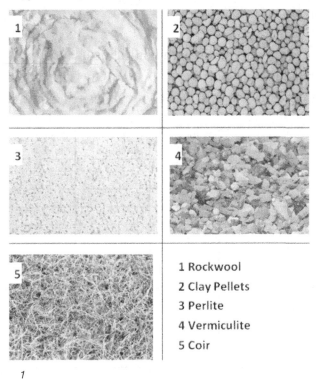

1 Rockwool
2 Clay Pellets
3 Perlite
4 Vermiculite
5 Coir

1

AGGREGATE MEDIUMS

This method is also referred to as the Aggregate Culture. Often, mediums are mixed to allow for a combination of needs. There may be a heavier medium at the bottom, such as small stones to provide weight and drainage. The main medium must provide stability for the plant to stand in a plant pot or small hanging basket.

Mixed in with that there must be a medium that can aerate well, such as perlite. Deeper rooted plants, such as chicory and beets, will need a system that has medium to support the heavier roots.

11. Roman023_photography. 2. Meister Photos. 3. Naramit. 4. Praisaeng. 5. Nastyaofly Shutterstock.com

Much is the same with top-heavy plants, such as squashes, zucchini, and even tomatoes.

It is a case of trial and error with your chosen system. What works for one gardener may not work for another. This book can guide you through the first stages, while you gain such experience.

Medium	Good Drainage	Water Retention	Oxygen Retention	Good Stability	Can Dry Out
*Rockwool Fiber *Melted Basalt	✓	✓	✓	✓	✓
*River Rock	✓	✗	✓	✓	✓
*Pumice	✓	✓	✓	✓	✓
*Clay Pellets *Hydrocorn *Hydroton	✓	✗	✓	✓	✓
*Sand	✓	✗	✗	✓	✓
*Composted Pine Bark	✓	✓	✓	✓	✓
*Coco Coir *Coco chips	✓	✓	✓	✓	✓
*Vermiculite	✗	✓	✗	✓	✗
*Perlite	✓	✗	✓	✓	✗

The above table points out some of the main points of each medium. Now, we will look in finer detail at which medium might work better with specific hydroponic systems.

DRIP SYSTEM

A system that works well with many plants, it can also be compatible with many different types of medium. The Drip System fares better with larger plants that retain the moisture for longer. With this system, a slow draining type of medium is best. Be aware that if not properly maintained the liquid nutrients may clog the feed pipes.

You can lessen this problem by using a filter, particularly if you are recycling or recovering your water system. It is advisable to flush out the pipes with plain, fresh water and cleaning fluids, periodically, to stop this from occurring.

- **Rockwool**

Rockwool is available as a slab, small block, or loose fiber, depending on the planter pots and trays you have. Keep the medium covered with a protective layer to discourage algae growth. Such growth flourishes in the light. It is best to set the drippers intermittently as this medium is prone to flooding if over-irrigated. Allow the roots to dry out a little in-between the water feeding process, which is good for the flowering and fruiting process.

- **Clay Pellets**

Excellent used with the Drip System, clay pellets are not prone to flooding because the pellets are so porous, so the roots cannot become saturated. Because of the spherical shape of the pellets, it is a good aerating method, as oxygen becomes trapped between the pellets. If growing vegetables, it is preferable to use a constant drip cycle during the daytime. However, if growing fruit or flowers, a timed on/off cycle of 15 minutes each during the daytime is better.

- **Vermiculite and Perlite**

Originally vermiculite contained asbestos fibers which can be harmful to your health. Now, modern products contain no asbestos. However, be wary of using older versions. It is more lightweight than perlite but they are both porous, so water and air flows through both mediums. Plus, they can both retain water for a while when the pump is off. Both are considered good for this system as they are porous and allow for a good airflow.

EBB AND FLOW

Because this system requires you to flood your feed trays, a heavier medium that will not float away is required. Avoid lightweight mediums. Your medium should have a good Water Holding Capacity (WHC), and High Air Filled Porosity (AFD).

With Ebb and Flow, your crop can take advantage of a mix of mediums. For example, coir retains water well, and clay pellets are good for drainage, so the two combined will allow both good drainage and moisture retention. A recommendation would be approximately 20% coir and 80% clay, so the coir does not retain too much water. It also means that should you have a system failure, each plant has a small amount of water in storage.

- **Rockwool** (See description above)

- **Coir**

A great substitute for peat moss because it is more sustainable. It does not rot easily as it contains natural allergens. It retains water like a sponge. However, the coir needs to be completely decomposed, otherwise, it can rob the plant of nutrients as it decomposes. If the coir is grown near salt water, it can also retain the salt. It may also have a high pH balance which can be too acidic for certain types of plants. It holds air well and it can be re-used so long as it is not contaminated with any pests or water bacteria. It may contain a natural fungus which will help plants fight off fungi although this will not be the case if the coir has been sterilized.

- **Clay Pellets**

The greatest asset of clay is the rich supply of oxygen that the pellets can hold, causing roots to grow at a fast rate. Ideally, soak the pellets before potting to allow for expansion. For the germination of seeds, you could crush the pellets a little to make the water retention more efficient. Clay pellets will hold nutrients for longer because of the binding process. This can cause a whitish substance to grow on the pellets which is salt. To avoid any toxic build-up, it is best to flush it out with plain water periodically. The pellets should never be allowed to dry out nor should they be constantly flooded. You need a fine balance. This is why they are ideal for the Ebb and Flow System.

- **Perlite**

Some might be a little nervous of using this medium, as it is made up of volcanic glass shards. However, it is heated until it expands into popcorn sized balls or smaller. It is non-organic and is often added to soil to aerate it better. It is a porous medium, allowing for good drainage. It serves well as an aerator medium. It is usually best mixed with another medium if it is being used for stability because it is lightweight.

NUTRIENT FILM TECHNIQUE

Whilst most NFT systems do not require any medium, fruiting and flowering plants do not do so well with their roots constantly wet. It is better to hang the plant in a medium so the nutritional water can be soaked up in between the water flow. This gives the roots the opportunity to dry out a little. The best mediums in these circumstances would be ones that soak up well, such as

- **Rockwool** (See description above)

- **Coir** (See description above)

For other plants that do not require such a "dry-out," it is better to try and ensure the roots do not become tangled by using:

- **Hanging Baskets**

This requires no mediums because the roots are suspended in a hanging basket, sitting in a tray, with holes for the baskets.

WATER CULTURE

This requires no mediums because the roots are suspended in water.

AEROPONICS

This requires no mediums because the roots are suspended in the air.

WICK IRRIGATION

- **Coir** (See description above)

- **Perlite** (See description above)

- **Clay Pellets** (See description above)

LIQUID CULTURE

There are hydroponic systems that require no medium at all, which are known as Liquid Culture systems. The plant roots are suspended into the nutrient-rich water. This includes the NFT, Aeroponics, and Water Culture systems. Smaller rooted plants, such as herbs, and fast-growing roots such as lettuce, are ideal for Liquid Culture. Also, plants with shallow roots, for instance strawberries.

NUTRIENTS FOR THE HYDROPONIC GARDEN

Since hydroponic systems don't use soil, the nutrients added to the water must contain all the minerals plants need to thrive. The selection of the appropriate nutrient solution is one of the most important decisions of your hydroponic plan. Healthy plant growth depends on having the right balance of nutrients.

There are 16 essential elements that plants need. These elements are absorbed by the plant in different ways. Some are transferred to the plant through the roots, while others are taken in through the pores of the leaf. Carbon, Oxygen, and Hydrogen, three of the most necessary, are available in both air and water. These need to be monitored and balanced. One common problem in hydroponics is a lack of sufficient carbon dioxide.

The next big three elements, Nitrogen, Phosphorus, and Potassium, are provided in the fertilizer nutrient blends made for growing hydroponic plants. A fine balance of these is extremely important. This is often referred to as the N-P-K mix. When looking at bottles or bags of fertilizer, you'll see a list of three numbers on the front, separated by dashes. It will look something like this: 3-4-1. These three numbers refer to the Nitrogen, Phosphorus, and Potassium (N-P-K) proportions of the mix.

Calcium, Magnesium, and Sulfur are the next most essential elements. They are also supplied by fertilizer supplements. Calcium is provided through a calcium nitrate ($CaNO3$) fertilizer. Magnesium and Sulfur are available with a magnesium sulfate ($MgSO4$) supplement.

The remaining 7 essential elements, Copper, Zinc, Boron, Molybdenum, Iron, Manganese, and Chlorine, are rarely deficient. If there is an Iron deficiency, you can supplement your plants with chelated iron.

To make sure your plants get everything they need, specially crafted fertilizer mixes are made for hydroponic crops. These mixes can be added to the water in your reservoir and distributed to your plants through the hydroponic system. Specific fertilizers are created for specific crops. They're not all interchangeable. The hydroponic nutrient mix for tomatoes will be quite different from the one for lettuce.

Nutrient mixes are available as liquid or granules. Liquid fertilizer is easy to use. You just pour it into the water reservoir as per the bottle's instructions. The downside to using liquid fertilizer is that it is more expensive and bulkier to store. Granulated fertilizer is more cost effective, easier to store, and often comes in bulk. However, it isn't as easy to use because it has to be mixed prior to use and it doesn't always dissolve completely. Either one will work fine, so it's a matter of personal preference and what's required by your particular system.

Granulated mixes are available in three types. The one-part mixes are simple and straight-forward. The fertilizer is mixed as indicated on the bag. These are simple to use, but not the best for making stock solutions. Some nutrients in high concentration will form solids. A multi-part solution is better for making stock solutions because the compounds are kept separately. They are relatively easy to mix, too. This is the most common choice for growers who are using granulated nutrient mixes. However, the multi-part mixes can be expensive, so it isn't the best choice unless you have a very large garden operation.

Hydroponic fertilizer mixes are also specialized for different stages of growth. They will indicate on the package the stage of growth for which they are designed. Examples of growth stages include vegetative (leaf growth) or blooming (flowering). You'll want to know what you actually want from the plant. Spinach, lettuce, and kale, for example, will benefit most from vegetative growth because you harvest the leaves of the plant. For plants that deliver a fruit or flower, you'll want to use the vegetative mix up to the point where you want them to flower. Then, switch to the flowering mix.

Nutrients are further classified based on the growing medium that is being used. The majority of nutrient mixes are made for a specific growing medium. Pay attention to package specifics and do your homework. If you're using a vermiculite mix but your growth medium is clay pellets, then you won't get optimal results. If the package doesn't give you all the details you need, then a simple online search will lead you in the right direction.

Hydroponic nutrients can be organic or synthetic. Organic fertilizers are best for systems that recirculate or reuse the nutrient solution. However, these mixes often include materials that can clog up sprayers, drip lines, and pumps. Synthetic nutrients don't have this issue and are therefore more commonly used in hydroponic systems. Organic fertilizers will often have a lower N-P-K listing than synthetic options. However, this doesn't mean they are of a lower quality. Synthetic mixes are generally fast-release, as opposed to the slow-release of organic, and so the readily available N-P-K is higher in the synthetic. However, organic mixes will deliver a natural, time release fertilizer that won't burn your roots.

NUTRIENTS YOU NEED FOR YOUR HYDROPONIC SYSTEM

- An N-P-K mix, formulated for the crop you are growing
- Calcium Nitrate (CaNO3)
- Magnesium Sulfate (MgSO4)

Adding Nutrients to Your Hydroponic System

1. Mix the solution as per the package instructions and add it to your reservoir.

2. Check your pH balance on a daily or weekly basis. (This timing will depend on the system you are using and the crops you are growing.)

3. Change out or top off your solution weekly or bi-weekly. (Again, the timing depends on the system and crops).

4. Flush your crop before harvesting. (Flushing your hydroponic crop means allowing it to grow without nutrient solution for a brief period prior to harvesting.)

What to Watch Out For

Even with a premix nutrient, issues can still arise. This is often due to an incorrect strength, usually because of over dilution. Other problems may occur when you use a dry mix and dissolve it in the water yourself. The result of an incorrect balance will be a mineral deficiency in your plants. Follow the manufactures recommendations carefully using an accurate tool for the measurements.

Signs of mineral deficiency could include:

- Yellowing of leaves
- Stunted growth
- Wilted or blackened leaves
- Swollen or discolored root tips.

Whichever option you prefer, the solution must maintain a constant temperature within the range of 70-80F/21-26C. This is to ensure optimal growth for your plants.

Lertwit Sasipreyajun/Shutterstock.com

TESTING THE PH

pH is the balance of acidity and alkalinity of your water. The nutrients you add to your water will influence the acid/alkaline balance. pH is measured on a scale from 0-14, with 0 being the most acidic and 14 being the most alkaline or basic. pH tests will tell you how well the plants will be able to use the nutrients. Each plant prefers a specific pH balance, and your plants won't be able to absorb the needed nutrients if the pH is too high or too low. Measure the pH after you've added the nutrients and then adjust as needed. A good baseline is to keep it between 5.5 and 6.5.

pH testing devices include paper litmus test strips, liquid test kits, and electronic testing pens. Paper test strips are the cheapest way to go, but they lack accuracy. Litmus strips change color when you dip them in solution. The resultant color reflects the pH. But checking the resulting color against the chart is a bit subjective, so you won't be able to determine the acidity of the solution with any amount of precision. The results can also be skewed if your nutrient solution isn't clear, which is a problem because many nutrient solutions will color the water.

Liquid test kits offer a fair balance of cost and precision. To use a liquid test kit, you take a small sample of solution and place it into a vial which contains a pH-sensitive dye. As with the litmus test, you will compare the resulting color with a chart. This will help you to determine the pH balance of your solution. The color changes are easier to see, and the test is a bit more sensitive than a litmus test, so the liquid test kit is somewhat more accurate. However, liquid test kits can also be skewed by the color of your solution (if it's not clear), so they aren't 100% accurate. However, unless your plants are extremely sensitive, liquid test kits are accurate enough.

If your number one consideration is accuracy in pH testing, digital meters are the way to go. They are more expensive, but they will tell you the pH to a tenth, and they won't be skewed by the color of your nutrient solution. To use a digital meter, you just insert the tip of the meter in the solution and it will provide you with a digital reading. The one thing you have to watch out for with these meters is calibration. To calibrate them, you must dip them in a pH neutral solution to provide a baseline. This is easier than it sounds, and you can find plenty of information about it online if you need it.

If you need to adjust the pH, phosphoric acid will raise acidity (lower pH) and lemon juice will lower acidity (raise pH). There are also a number of pH adjustment products readily available in hydroponic stores.

FLUSHING

The nutrients you feed your plants build up in them and can cause bitter or chemical tastes. Flushing out the plants before harvesting ensures a good end product. Do this for 4-7 days prior to the harvest. The most traditional way to do this is to irrigate your plants with pure water and allow them to process it through their system for up to a week before harvesting. If you'd like to get fancy, several flushing agents are readily available at hydroponic stores. They'll speed up the process and ensure a complete flush. Remember – flushing is extremely important. You'll be able to taste the difference, regardless of what it is you're growing.

OPTIONAL ADDITIVES FOR THE PLANTS

Bloom Maximizers

These are added to your nutrient solution to increase the size and yield of your plants. They are usually high in Phosphorus and Potassium. This additive can be quite expensive, but it's generally worth the price for the boost it gives the plants. Nutrient burn can be a problem when using this so monitor the plants closely if you choose to use it. (Nutrient burn is the plant's equivalent of chemical burn. If you see the roots turn a different color, take on an unhealthy texture, or shrivel after adding the solution, flush the reservoir with pure water so that the plants can recover. It's far better, though, to make sure that you use the right concentration and you don't have to resort to damage control.) Bloom maximizers should only be used during the flowering stage of growth.

Mycorrhizae and Other Fungi

Mycorrhizae are small fungal filaments that penetrate the roots, increasing their surface area. They also gather and break down certain nutrients. Mycorrhizae exist in a symbiotic relationship with nearly all plant species. They help plants to absorb nutrients and water. In return, they receive some of the sugars that plants create through photosynthesis.

Mycorrhizal fungi can be added directly to the nutrient solution and will grow alongside the roots as they do in nature. You can also add other fungi such as Trichoderma to aid in breaking down nutrients and making your crops more resistant to soil pests. Trichoderma and Mycorrhizal fungi are readily available in hydroponics stores. They will help your plants to remain healthy and grow more quickly.

Vitamins and Enzymes

Thiamine (vitamin B-1) supports and strengthens the immune system of plants so they can better withstand stress and disease. It also facilitates root development, making the plants more resistant to shock and helping them to take in nutrients more quickly. This is especially important when transplanting. Enzymes break down nutrients, making them easier for plants to absorb. They are also helpful for preventing algae growth.

Root Stimulators

Root stimulators are compounds that replicate the benefits of natural soil. There are beneficial microbes in soil that promote plant growth, just as there are harmful microbes that interfere with plant growth. Rooting stimulators introduce the healthy microbes into your hydroponics system, helping your plants to have stronger immune systems, more access to nitrogen, and faster root development. They are also excellent at preventing bacterial complications in the root structure.

Overall, root stimulators promote fast, healthy plant growth. If you add root stimulators at the beginning of your growing cycle, they will continue to reproduce throughout your plants growth from seedling to harvest, providing more robust, faster-growing crops from the start.

NUTRIENT NOTES

When searching for nutrients, you will encounter a slew of brands and products. While they'll all claim to be the best, there's a great deal of variety in quality from one brand to the next, even among products designed for the same purpose. A brand or company might be good for one thing, but not so great for another.

The best way to deal with this is to read reviews from several growers to find out which products they prefer. This will provide you with solid feedback from people who have been there. Find hydroponic forums where you can post the details of your system and crop. You'll get plenty of responses from experienced growers that will direct you to products that have worked for them in similar situations.

Water quality is of utmost importance in a hydroponic system. Do not underestimate the necessity of good clean water. Distilled or RO (reverse osmosis) water is the best choice. Tap water or city water can have pollutants, chemicals, additives, and any number of things that can potentially have a negative impact on plant growth. This being said, plants use *lots* of water. If your prime concern is economy, then you'll use what you've got. Just remember that you get out of the plant what you put into it.

TYPES OF LIGHTING

Plants needs around twelve hours of light per day. Of course, this will vary depending on the plant that you are growing. Some plants prefer a great deal of light, while others do quite well with only a moderate amount. Remember that plants get their energy from light. If your hydroponic system isn't in a place where it is getting natural light from the sun, you'll need to set up a lighting system.

Plants have rhythms, just like we do. Look into the preferred light cycles of your plants, and set up timers so that you give them a schedule as close as possible to their natural cycle. The optimal light schedule will differ depending on the growth stage of the plant as well. Many plants grow well vegetatively when provided with constant light, but need cycles of light and darkness to trigger flowering.

Maciej/Shutterstock.com

The type of lighting you need depends on a wide variety of factors specific to your system: enclosure type, plant type, system size, ventilation, and last but not least, budget. Fluorescent tubes are good for a single low-budget system. Small systems will fare better with CFLs (Compact Fluorescent Lamps). These lights were designed as an efficient alternative to incandescent bulbs. They screw into a standard socket and provide sufficient light, but you may want to arrange reflectors so that the light is focused on the plant.

HIDs (High Intensity Discharge lamps) are another option. They are a bit more costly than CFLs, but they are a preferred lighting option for experienced growers. This is because they have a very high light output and are four to eight times more efficient than standard incandescent bulbs. However, they produce a lot of heat, so you'll have to ventilate your system to prevent it from drying out.

Another option is to use LEDs (Light Emitting Diode lamps). This is the high-tech option and will cost quite a bit more at the beginning, but they use a fraction of the electricity of other options and produce less heat. LEDs can also be calibrated to produce the exact spectrum of light that your plant needs. If you only plan to grow one crop, it's probably not worth it to purchase LEDs. But, if this is the beginning of a long relationship with hydroponic growing, they will more than pay off in the long run.

Fluorescent Lights

Fluorescent lights are available in a wide range of sizes and spectrums. They are not ideal for large plants but they will work. They are generally inexpensive, easy to set up, and will work in a pinch.

Compact Fluorescent Bulbs

These are a good choice because they aren't too expensive and they don't require any special wiring or set-up (they screw into a regular light socket). They produce light in all directions and are best used with a reflector so you don't waste any heat or light.

High-Intensity Discharge (HID) Lights

HID lights have a high light output and are a preferred choice for growers. Using HIDs will be better for your plants than fluorescents and less expensive than incandescent bulbs in the long run. At the same time, they are expensive, require a special set-up, and need ventilation because of their high heat output.

LED Lights

LED lights can provide the exact spectrum of light your plant needs. They last longer than all other lights and use less electricity. The upfront cost, however, is imposing. As mentioned above, LEDs are worth it if you plan to be growing many crops over the years. For a one-off, though, you may be better off with a different option.

CHAPTER 5: PLANTS FOR HYDROPONIC GARDENING

There is a whole range of plants that can be grown using hydroponic gardening. Most plants can be grown using any of the hydroponic methods. There are some which do better with a specific system. However, they will all do far better than if they were grown by the traditional soil method.

Now that you have a better understanding of the various hydroponic gardening systems, as well as the mediums and nutrients to use, you will need to decide which plants you want to grow.

If you are a beginner, it is better to start with the smaller rooted plants, such as herbs. Large rooted plants can pose problems, such as blockages, that the novice may not realize are happening.

BEST PLANTS TO GROW WITH YOUR HYDROPONIC SYSTEM

Bayuuafif /Shutterstock.com

As a rule of thumb, you can grow pretty much any vegetable or herb using the hydroponic system. Many fruits do well too, as do flowers. Often it can be a case of trial and error before you find the best system and crop that suits your own environment. As mentioned previously in this book, much is dependent on your available space, budget, time and energy.

What works for one grower may not work for another. Those who grow in a greenhouse or outdoors may find their crops more susceptible to pests. If growing in a room in your home, then it won't be such an issue because the plants are better protected. Other factors, such as nutrients, pH levels, temperature, humidity, lighting, and ventilation, all play their role in hydroponic growing.

This following section will give you a general idea of the types of edible plants that are best to grow in each of the various systems.

Growing a wide variety of flowers, such as tulips, can be done on a small scale for personal use. Any seasonal species can be grown all year around.

GETTING STARTED

Beeboys/Shutterstock.com

If you are keen to grow edible plants, then go with those that are known to do well without needing too much attention. When you are limited by space and experience, try beginning with the Wick System, whereby you can build a smaller hydroponic garden. The following suggestions are fast growing, quite hardy, and do not need a lot of space.

Vegetable: Spinach, Bell Peppers, Lettuce, Tomatoes

Fruit: Strawberries

Herbs: Basil, Parsley

Have a look at the following table as a rough guide to what grows best with each system.

Method	Vegetables	Fruits	Herbs
Drip System: better suited for larger plants	Lettuce, Pumpkins, Peppers, Leeks, Onions, Peas, Radishes, Cucumbers, Zucchini, Squashes, Green Beans	Melons, Strawberries, Tomatoes	Rosemary, Basil, Chives, Oregano
Ebb and Flow	Eggplant, Lettuce, Peas, Peppers, Spinach, Tomatoes, Cucumber	Tomatoes	Anise, Basil, Chamomile, Dill, Chives, Fennel, Cilantro, Lavender, Coriander, Mint, Oregano, Rosemary, Parsley, Thyme, Sage, Tarragon. Watercress
Nutrient Film Technique	Lettuce, Spinach, Bell Peppers	Strawberries, Tomatoes Blueberries	Basil, Sage
Deep Water Culture	Radish, Lettuce, Kale, Cabbage, Broccoli	Water Melon (but needs added support)	Most herbs can be grown in Deep Water Culture
Wick System: ideally, plants that don't produce fruit i.e. greens and herbs	Lettuce, Watercress	Not suitable for fruit	Most herbs grow well in a Wick System
Aeroponics	Lettuce, Eggplant	Tomatoes, Water Melon	Mint, Mustard Seed, Ginger

SEASONED GROWER

For the experienced gardener, you could be adventurous and consider growing plants that need more attention and space. Look into growing with an Aeroponics system and start plants that have larger roots. It is better to have a larger system for more advanced plants. Root and tuber vegetables, such as carrots, parsnips, and even potatoes, that would normally grow with their roots underground, will need much more attention and space.

For those with a larger hydroponic garden, you could advance to the more difficult crops, such as zucchini, or even vine plants, but they do need space. When you become more experienced, you could consider growing sunflowers, tobacco, shrubs, nut trees, and even the prickly blackberry shrub.

READY TO GO

Now that you have studied some of the basic needs of each hydroponic system, I hope you feel you have enough information to pick the right hydroponic system and suitable crops for you.

There will be hurdles along the way; any type of growing is not without its own set of problems. If you are aware of the pitfalls, then you will be ready to counter them should they happen. Whether you decide to start with a large or a small hydroponic system, there is no need to break your back digging up soil.

My first tip to you is to start with small rooted and quick growing plants, such as lettuce or herbs. That way, you will be quick to reap the benefits of your labor of love. That first crop will spur you on to bigger and better things. The advantage of hydroponics is that you will yield a crop quickly, so long as you do it right. I hope you are spurred on by my own enthusiasm and feel encouraged to get started.

GLOSSARY

Acid

A solution with a pH level of below 7.

Aeration

The process of circulating air through a substance or liquid, to provide the roots with oxygen.

Aeroponics

A method of growing plants hydroponically, by allowing roots to suspend in the air and receive a mist of liquid nutrients at timed intervals.

Aggregate

An inert material used as a growing medium.

Agriculture

Cultivation of crops and livestock for farming.

Air stone

Holds oxygen to help aerate water solution.

Algae

Single-celled plant growth. Grows from excess minerals caused by overfeeding plants.

Alkaline

A nutrient solution, or growing medium, with a pH level higher than 7.

Aquaponics

A symbiotic relationship between the breeding of fish, and growth of plants in water.

Bloom Booster

A nutrient with a high concentration of phosphorus used to increase the bloom yield in flowers.

Burn

Yellow or brown leaf tips, due to excess salt or over fertilization.

Calcium (Ca)

Macronutrient that helps build plant cells to strengthen stems and roots.

Carbon Dioxide (CO2)

Gas present in the air, essential for plant life.

Clay Pellet

Baked clay growing medium.

Chlorine (CI)

A micronutrient that aids photosynthesis.

Chlorosis

Yellowing leaves due to imbalanced pH levels

Coco-Coir

Growing medium fiber extracted from the outer husk of a coconut.

Conditioning

A process to reduce pH levels in Rockwool medium.

Copper

Micronutrient essential for plant growth. Has anti-microbial attributes.

Cycle Timer

A tool to turn on and off at timed intervals. Used for devices such as pumps and feeding systems.

Deep Water Culture (DWC)

A method of growing plants hydroponically, where the roots are submerged in a nutritional water solution.

Drip System (Drip Emitter System)

A hydroponic method of growing plants. A solution of water and nutrients drip onto growing medium, at timed intervals.

Ebb and Flow (Flood & Drain)

A hydroponic method of growing plants. Growing medium is flooded with nutrient-enriched water, at timed intervals.

Electrical Conductivity (EC)

Water's ability to conduct electricity. Used in hydroponics to measure water salinity.

Fertilizer

Minerals for feeding plants.

Flushing

Cleaning out the water system with clear fresh water.

Foggers

A spraying system, used in Aeroponics.

Fungus

Parasitical organisms, such as mold, mildew, and yeasts that can cause damage to plants. .

Gravity Drain

The return drainage pipe, used in many hydroponic systems. Water flows with gravity.

Greenhouse

Structure for growing and protecting plants, made from glass or transparent plastic, on a frame.

Herbicide

Selective chemicals to kill certain types of plant life, ie weeds.

Horticulture

Plant cultivation.

Hydrocorn

Another term for clay pellets.

Hydroculture

Passive hydroponic method for growing plants. An inert growing medium is used instead of soil.

Hydroton

Another term for clay pellets.

Hydroponic

The process of growing plants without soil, using nutritional water solutions, and sometimes growing mediums.

Insecticides

A mix of chemicals that will kill insects.

Inert

Material that is chemically inactive.

Iron (Fe)

Micronutrient, important for photosynthesis.

Liquid Culture

Growing plants in a nutritional water solution, without the use of a medium.

Macronutrients

Group of nutrients to feed plants. Primary ones being - Nitrogen (N), Phosphorus (P) and Potassium (K).

Medium

Varying materials used to grow plants in, when not using soil.

Micronutrients

Present in nutrient solutions, in small amounts. Essential for plant growth.

Mineral solution

Nutrient enriched water for feeding plants.

Nitrogen (N)

Macronutrient that aids plant growth.

Nutrient Film Technique (NFT)

A hydroponic method of growing plants. Set on a slant with nutritional solution flowing through a gulley. Roots hang in a gulley.

Nutrients

Substances, or compounds, that make up food. Contains Macronutrients and Micronutrients.

Pests

Organisms that live off other organisms.

Potential Hydrogen (pH)

Levels of acidity and alkalinity in water

Phosphorus (P)

Macronutrient, essential element for plant growth.

Photosynthesis

A process of turning light into chemical energy. Mostly used by green plants.

Potassium (K)

Macronutrient, essential element for plant growth. Helps fight diseases and increase fruit growth.

Pumice

Growing medium made from crushed volcanic rock.

Recirculating

Re-using, or recycling, of nutrient-enriched water.

Reservoir Tank

A container that holds nutritional water.

Rockwool

Melted rock. Used as growing medium.

Sand

Inexpensive growing medium, widely available.

Suspended

Hanging roots, as in dangling in the air rather than settled in a medium.

Tray Container

A container that holds the plants.

Vermiculite

Heat expanded mineral. Pebble-shaped. Often combined with perlite.

Wick

A hydroponic method of growing plants. Absorbing wick draws water up from the nutrient-enriched water to feed the roots.

Wood Bark

Usually composted pine bark.

Zinc

Aids chlorophyll synthesis.

RICHARD BRAY

DO IT YOURSELF
HYDRO
PONICS

12 EASY AND AFFORDABLE WAYS
TO BUILD YOUR OWN HYDROPONIC SYSTEM

Chatree.l/Shutterstock.com

TABLE OF CONTENTS

CHAPTER 1: BUILD YOUR OWN HYDROPONIC SYSTEM

Note: Since the first book already provided an overview of the six hydroponic systems I will not get into detail again here. You can go back to page 8 if you need a refresher.

Now that you understand the basics of the six types of hydroponic systems, let's learn more about building them. The next six sections of this book go into specifics about each system. The components of each system are explained in detail along with variations and options. This guide will help you determine and create the ideal system for your growing needs. In each section, there is a step-by-step guide, with detailed explanation and illustrations of how to build the system along with a list of all the needed tools and materials.

HOW TO SET UP A WICKING SYSTEM

The Wicking System is the simplest hydroponic system and the easiest to set up. It takes very little planning or in-depth engineering to construct. It's the best method for beginners and also makes a great hands-on project for children. The wicking system is categorized as a passive system because it contains few moving parts. No special machinery or equipment, such as pumps or motors, are needed to keep the system operational.

Because of their basic design, Wicking Systems work best for plants that don't require a lot of monitoring or water and that are generally easier to grow. Herbs and vegetables like lettuce and other leafy greens are excellent choices for this method. Tomatoes and other fruiting vegetables are not ideal, as they require a great deal of water.

THE FOUR (OR FIVE) MAIN COMPONENTS OF A WICKING SYSTEM

- Wick

- Grow Tray

- Growing Medium

- Reservoir

- Aeration System (optional)

- **The Wick**

The centerpiece of this hydroponic set-up, and the source of its name, is the wick. The term wicking refers to a material's ability to absorb and transport liquid through a porous surface. Some common examples of wicking are the way in which a paper towel soaks up spilled juice from the floor and how fabrics soak up the sweat from your skin. It works because water molecules like to cling to one another in close cohesion. They also stick to other surfaces in the same way. The ability of a wick or tube to transport water is known as capillary action. In this case, the wicking material absorbs water and nutrients, transporting them to the roots of your plants.

A wick can be made of or re-purposed from a variety of different materials. Fibrous rope, rayon rope, yarn, felt, nylon rope, and strips of fabric from old clothing or blankets all make excellent wicks. Two things to consider when choosing a wicking material are the rate at which it absorbs water and its ability to withstand rotting. To test the wicking ability of your chosen material, or to test the wicking of several different materials against one another, place the ends of each in a container of dyed water and monitor how far the colored water travels up the cloth in an hour.

The shorter your wick, the quicker it will deliver water and nutrients to your plants. It is best to situate your plants right above the reservoir if possible. Each plant will have at least one wick, possibly two, depending on what you're growing.

- **The Grow Tray**

In this method, you plant seeds in a grow tray which holds the growing medium. It can be just one pot or a tray that holds several plants, depending on how big a system you want to build and what you are growing.

- **The Growing Medium**

Since the water will be delivered at a slow speed by the wicking material, it's best to choose a growing medium that absorbs and holds water very well. Ideal choices for this include vermiculite, perlite, and coconut coir.

Another good choice is a soilless potting mix. A soilless potting mix is composed primarily of sphagnum peat moss. It is inexpensive, lightweight, holds water plentifully and at the same time, drains well. Soilless potting mixes often blend peat moss with coconut coir, bark, or vermiculite.

Whichever growing medium you decide to use, it is important to flush it out every few weeks with fresh water to prevent a build-up of nutrients. If the nutrients are allowed to accumulate to high concentrations, they can become toxic to your plants.

- **The Reservoir**

Water and nutrients are stored in the reservoir. The bottom of the wick is suspended in the nutrient-enriched water of the reservoir and transports it to your plants. The reservoir doesn't have to be complicated or fancy. However, it's preferable that the container be dark in color because light will encourage algae growth.

If you are using a container that is see-through, either paint it a dark color to prevent light from entering or create a shade to place around it. The second option is preferable, especially if you make it removable. This allows you to keep it in place during the growing cycles and remove it when checking water and nutrient levels.

It is important to keep the reservoir filled, as the wicks are more effective when the water has less distance to travel. If the reservoir gets low, then the water has further to travel and your plants won't be receiving the correct level of hydration. Lower hydration levels can slow the growth of your plants.

Please see the Water Culture section to determine the recommended size for your reservoir.

- **Optional Aeration Device**

To refine your Wicking Hydroponic garden and make it more efficient, you may choose to include an aeration system. Aeration systems ensure that the water has enough oxygen in it to promote healthy plant growth. Your plants will still receive oxygen from the air without such a system, but they can absorb oxygen more easily from their roots. By aerating the water, you'll promote quick and healthy plant growth. You can make an effective and inexpensive aeration system with no more than an aquarium air stone and pump.

HOW TO MAKE A WICKING HYDROPONIC SYSTEM

This design is for a basic system with only a few plants. You can expand on it as far as you like. If you want to grow many plants, simply get a large grow tray and large reservoir. For just one plant, use a pot and a small reservoir. A great way to start is to build a small system at first to let you get a feel for the process. Once you are comfortable with that, you can expand the system or build a larger one.

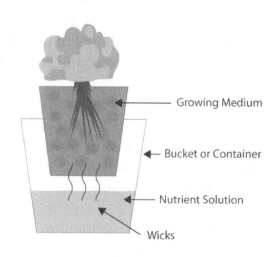

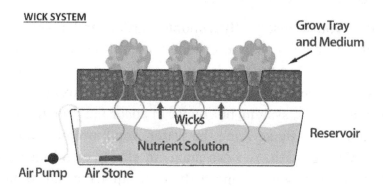

Illus. 1 – Small and Large Wick System Set-Up

What You Will Need:

- Grow tray – it can be a tray for several plants or a pot for one plant

- Growing medium

- Two strips of wicking material per plant

- Reservoir

- Nutrient solution

- Aeration system (Optional) [air pump, air stone, tubing]

Assembly:

1. Fill the grow tray or pot with the growing medium.

2. Arrange the wicks in the growing medium so they hang down far enough to reach the reservoir. If your grow tray does not have holes in it, you will need to cut some to fit the wicks.

3. Space your seedlings out in the growing medium.

4. Fill your reservoir with water and nutrients.

5. Arrange the grow tray on top of the reservoir so that the wicks dip into the nutrient water solution.

6. Congratulations, you've made a wicking hydroponic system!

7. If you want to add the oxygen system, connect the tubing to the air stone. Place the air stone in the reservoir. Attach the other end of the tubing to the air pump (the pump DOES NOT go in the water). Turn on the pump and make sure the air stone is producing bubbles.

How to Turn a Liter Soda Bottle Into a Wicking Hydroponic System

There are several different methods you can use to build your own system. The simplest, and a favorite in classrooms around the country, is the soda bottle method.

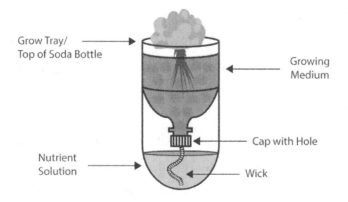

Grow Tray/
Top of Soda Bottle

Growing
Medium

Cap with Hole

Nutrient
Solution

Wick

Illus. 2 – Soda Bottle Wick System

What You Will Need:

- 1 clean plastic 2-liter soda bottle, with cap
- Scissors
- Rubber bands
- Duct Tape
- Wicking material
- Growing medium
- Nutrient solution

Assembly:

1. Cut the soda bottle 8" from the top.
2. Cover the cut edges of the bottle with duct tape to prevent slippage after assembly.

3. Cut a hole in the cap large enough to thread the wicking material through. Thread material into the hole so you have half the length of the wick on each side.

4. Mix the water and nutrient solution (according to package directions). Fill the base of the soda bottle to 4" from the bottom. You may need to add more or reduce the amount, depending on how far the inverted bottle goes down.

5. Invert the top of the bottle and fill with your growing medium, making sure the wick is weaved and stretched out through it.

6. Plant your seedling in the growing medium.

7. Fit the bottle top, cap side down, into the bottom half of the bottle. Make sure the wick is free to rest in the nutrient solution.

8. The bottle cap should be above the water level with the wick dangling down into the nutrients.

Caring For Your Plants in a Wicking System

- When the nutrient-enriched water solution gets low, replace it entirely with a new mix of water and nutrients.

- Flush the growing medium with fresh water every two weeks to prevent harmful nutrient buildup.

HOW TO SET UP A WATER CULTURE HYDROPONIC SYSTEM

The Water Culture system of hydroponics is commonly referred to as the purest hydroponic system, as it is entirely water-based. There is no growing medium used to hold the plants in place, and the roots of the plant are continuously immersed in aerated water.

The main benefit of using this type of system is that it is relatively inexpensive and easy to set up. Also, there are few moving parts that could be prone to break down. The downside is that because it is a small system, nutrient concentrations and water levels can fluctuate widely. There is a strong possibility of over- or under-compensating. A power outage or pump failure can also be an issue. If the pump is not continuously supplying oxygen, the plants can 'drown'.

The disadvantages of this system can be overcome by careful monitoring and maintenance. You'll want to check the system daily to make sure that everything is working properly.

THE FIVE MAIN COMPONENTS OF A WATER CULTURE SYSTEM

- Net Pot

- Reservoir

- Lid/Grow Tray

- Growing Medium

- Oxygen Pump System (Pump, Tubing, Air Stone)

- **Net Pot**

A net pot may sound a bit strange, but the name is self-explanatory. It is a small round plastic basket with holes in it that make it look like hard netting. The basket weave holds the plant so it doesn't fall into the reservoir, while the roots grow out through the holes. Net pots come in a variety of sizes to accommodate different sizes of plants and systems. Don't forget, the root system will become larger as your plants grow. You'll want to select a size that will accommodate this growth.

- **Reservoir**

The reservoir holds the water and nutrient solution and it won't need to be very deep. The ideal depth depends on what plants you are growing. For example, lettuce will flourish with a reservoir that holds four to six inches of water. To determine the appropriate depth, consider the length of the root system at full growth.

A common rookie mistake is to use a reservoir that is too small. It can be hard to imagine that such a little seed will grow to produce such a huge root system. Your plants will grow quickly with this system and the roots can outgrow a small container before you realize it. Switching containers halfway through the growing process can be both expensive and an unnecessary hassle. This can also damage your plants, so it's best to plan the correct setup from the beginning.

To make sure you select a reservoir large enough for your needs, consider what you plant in each pot and how many pots you'll set up in the reservoir. In the section on the raft method below, you'll see that these systems can contain quite a few plants. Consider the size of your plants at full growth, and then use this rule of thumb to determine reservoir size:

- For small plants, supply a minimum of a ½ gallon of water per plant

- For medium plants, supply a minimum of 1 ½ gallons of water per plant

- For large plants, supply a minimum of 2 ½ gallons of water, per plant

It is always best to err on the side of caution, so don't be worried about using a much larger container than you think you need. In fact, you may wish to choose a container double the expected size. Make sure to keep it filled with enough water to cover the roots, regardless of how much water is required per plant.

If you use a raft-type lid and a large container, it's helpful to mark the 1-, 2-, and 5- gallons points and so forth on the inside of the container with a permanent marker. This will help you to determine how much water you need to refill the reservoir as the levels drop. It will also make it easy to monitor how fast your plants are absorbing water.

If you use a bucket or another large container with a fitted lid, make sure to fill it high enough to keep the roots submerged. If you use a see-through reservoir, make sure to cover it with a removable shade. Any light entering your reservoir will break down the nutrient solution and encourage algae growth.

- **Lid/Grow Tray**

The lid is designed to cradle the net pot so it doesn't fall into the nutrient solution. It is usually a flat surface with a hole cut in the center. The hole should be large enough to fit the bottom half of the net pot, yet not so large that it allows the entire net pot to slip all the way through. It is then secured firmly to the reservoir to keep it in place.

Alternatively, you can use a floating raft. Styrofoam is the most common medium used to create a raft since it will float on top of the water reservoir and provide a buffer between the water and the upper portion of the plant. Multiple holes can be cut in the Styrofoam, angled slightly, and somewhat smaller than the size of the net pots. The goal is to suspend the net pots securely in place and prevent them from sliding through.

- **Growing Medium**

In the Water Culture System, no soil is needed. However, it is sometimes necessary to use a material to keep the seedling plant secure in the net pot while it grows. There are several choices for this. Rockwool is an excellent choice. It comes in cubes specially designed for hydroponic gardening. You can also use wood chips, packing peanuts (Styrofoam), vermiculite, perlite, coconut fiber, expanded clay pellets (grow rocks), rice hulls, or pumice.

Make sure the pieces of material are large enough that they won't slip through the holes in your net pot and fall into the reservoir. Also, it's preferable to choose a material that is resistant to mold or fungus. Fungus can damage the roots of your plants and endanger the crop.

- **Air Pump/Air Hose/Air Stone**

The air pump, hose, and stone work together to create an aeration system to oxygenate your nutrient solution. In a Water Culture System, the more air bubbles, the better. The bubbles need to make direct contact with the root systems to deliver oxygen. The water in the reservoir should look almost like it's boiling.

An aquarium air pump and air stone will work fine for this system. They are easy to find at pet stores or online. The pump is connected to the stone via the tubing. The pump drives air through the tube into the porous air stone. Small bubbles then stream upwards from the stone.

A soaker hose can be used in place of the air stone. Soaker hoses will produce small bubbles. These have a higher surface area by volume, delivering more oxygen for the same volume of air pumped through the medium. Put simply, the smaller the air bubbles, the better.

RECIRCULATING WATER CULTURE SYSTEM

Recirculating water culture systems connect several growing reservoirs to one central tank. You may wish, for example, to use five large buckets or storage containers. One will act as the controller bucket, while the other four contain plants in net pots. The buckets can then be linked in series, connected to one another with intake hoses and overflow tubes. The controller bucket will contain a large pump to drive the water in the system. Pond or fountain pumps are an ideal choice. The pump sends the water into the first bucket in the series, which then overflows into the next, and so on. The final bucket overflows back into the controller bucket to recirculate the nutrient solution.

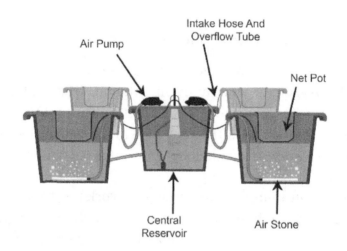

Illus. 3 – Recirculating Water Culture System

This method is often used by large commercial growers. The advantage of this approach is that growers only need to check water and nutrient levels of the controller container. However, the water is not aerated as completely as it is in other systems. This results in slower plant growth.

DEEP WATER CULTURE SYSTEM

This term is often used as if it is completely different from a Water Culture System. However, the only difference is that in a deep water culture system (DWC), the water in the reservoir is deeper than 8".

What You Will Need:

- An airtight glass aquarium

- Material for a light shield (aluminum or cardboard work great)

  - If you would like to monitor root growth, make your light shield removable.

- Floating platform –1½" to 2" thick layers of Styrofoam are ideal. Cut the raft to fit loosely inside the reservoir.

- Net pots to hold the plants. You could also use a small plastic cup with tapered sides. Simply cut holes to allow the roots to grow through.

- Growing medium of choice (Expanded clay pebbles are recommended to keep seedlings in place)

- Aeration system (air pump, air stone, tubing to connect them)

- Nutrients (see the chapter on choosing nutrient solutions for your hydroponic garden)

- pH test kit (Optional yet highly recommended. They are inexpensive and absolutely worth the cost.)

Assembly:

- Cut holes in your Styrofoam floating platform to fit your net pots. Make sure the holes are smaller than the net pots so they don't fall through. The bottom of the cups should hang just below the Styrofoam.

- Add growing medium to each of the pots. If the medium begins to fall out of the holes, you can place a small piece of cloth over the holes first. Set aside.

- Fill the reservoir/aquarium with water. You can always add or remove water if necessary.

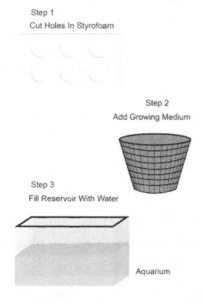

Illus. 4 – Aquarium Water Culture System Set-Up

- Mix nutrients as per package instructions and add to the water.

- Test your pH and adjust the nutrients accordingly. Different plants require a different pH. To check different pH requirements for plants see <u>Appendix II - Hydroponic Plants pH</u>

- Attach tubing to the air stone and place it in the water.

- Attach the free end of the tubing to the air pump (the air pump DOES NOT go in the water) and situate it on the side of the reservoir.

- Plug in the pump and make sure that the air stone is producing bubbles.

- Arrange the floating platform on top of the water.

- Put your seedlings in the net pots, secured gently by the growing medium.

- Put each pot in its hole in the platform. The bottom of the pots (i.e. the plant's roots) should be submerged in the water. Be careful not to submerge the stem.

- Congratulations, you've created a water-based hydroponic system!

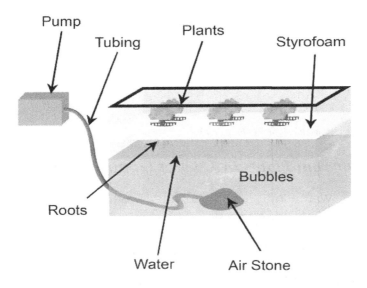

Illus. 5 – Side View: Aquarium Water Culture Set-Up

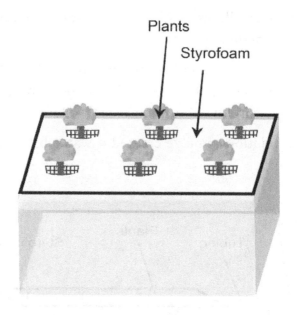

Plants

Styrofoam

Illus. 6 – Top View: Aquarium Water Culture System

Caring For Your Plants In A Water Culture System:

- Add water only (no nutrients!) when the plants have absorbed half of the solution.

- Check your pH levels and adjust only if needed

- The second time the plants have absorbed half the solution in the reservoir (approximately every 1-2 weeks, depending on what you're growing), it is time to refresh the nutrient solution. Drain the reservoir completely and blend a fresh batch of nutrients and water.

HOW TO TURN A 5-GALLON BUCKET INTO A DEEP WATER CULTURE (DWC) HYDROPONIC SYSTEM

What You Will Need:

- Five-gallon bucket with lid

- Net pot or another container with tapered sides and holes cut in it for roots to grow through

- Aeration system (air pump, air stone, tubing to connect them)

- Growing medium

- Nutrients

- pH test kit

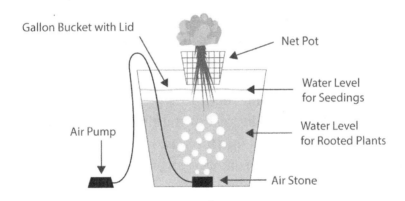

Gallon Bucket with Lid

Net Pot

Water Level for Seedings

Air Pump

Water Level for Rooted Plants

Air Stone

Illus. 7 – 5-Gallon Bucket Water Culture System Set-Up

Assembly:

Follow the instructions listed above for the aquarium set-up. The only difference is that instead of cutting a hole for your net pot in Styrofoam, you will be cutting a hole in the lid of your 5-gallon bucket. Remember to make the hole smaller than the pot so the pot doesn't slip through.

How to Set Up an Ebb and Flow Hydroponic System

Though this system looks complicated on paper, once you set it up and see it in action, you'll see that it's one of the simplest designs. Ebb and flow systems are easy to manage and can be adapted to fit any space, as large or as small as you like, and any shape you desire. You'll need a timer and a fill/drain overflow fitting kit, but these are easy to find at any hardware store. You'll also need a drill to put holes in the growing container and reservoir. This system is quite versatile, making it a popular choice for home gardeners.

The basic mechanics of an Ebb and Flow System are as follows: Plants are housed on a grow tray which is attached with tubing to a reservoir. The pump is on a timer and floods the grow tray with nutrient-solution several times a day. The flooding time is typically a minute, after which time the pump turns off. Gravity drains the water back into the reservoir through the pump. An overflow drain is also set up to ensure all water returns to the reservoir.

In this method, the plant roots are flooded for several short periods during the day. The rest of the time, they'll be out of the water and exposed to oxygen. This way, both oxygen and nutrient absorption are optimized promoting strong plant growth.

THE SEVEN MAIN COMPONENTS OF AN EBB AND FLOW SYSTEM

- Grow Tray
- Reservoir
- Growing Medium
- Fill/Drain Overflow Fitting Kit
- Pump
- Tubing

- Timer

- **Grow Tray & Reservoir**

These are listed together because, in most designs of this type of system, the grow tray and reservoir are connected. The size of one will determine the size of the other. In the stacked container design, the grow tray will fit snugly into the reservoir. Alternately, the grow tray can sit on a separate table. For this design, the size of growing tray and reservoir do not need to be matched so closely. Regardless of which setup you use, the grow tray must be above the reservoir for the pump to operate correctly and create the ebb and flow.

There are two basic types of grow tray arrangement. The first uses a single grow tray which has all the plants in one place without separation. The entire tray gets flooded with the nutrient solution at the same time. The benefit of this design is that it is easier to assemble. The downside is that the plants can't be moved around easily. This system can be set up using the stacked-container arrangement or with a separate table to set the grow tray on.

The second type of grow tray system uses individual growing containers for each plant. These containers are placed in a tray which gets flooded with nutrient solution. This design can support many plants and the grow container can become very heavy. Because of this, it's best to support the grow container by placing it on a table rather than using the stacked container design.

When planning the size of your grow tray, consider the space that you have available and how many plants you want to grow. Reservoir size will be dependent upon space and upon how many plants you want to water. The key is to ensure there is enough water to flood the grow tray. Smaller reservoirs also require more frequent nutrient top-ups. As the plants grow larger, they will use up water and nutrients more quickly. A small reservoir will do the job while plants are still small, but it's better to overestimate reservoir size than to underestimate. Your plants may grow very large, and faster than you may expect.

Please see the Water Culture section to determine the ideal size for your reservoir.

The stacked container arrangement is commonly used for an Ebb and Flow System because it makes the best use of space. It consists of one large plastic container as a reservoir (for example, a 20-gallon storage bin), and a smaller container of the same length and width, yet shorter in height, to serve as the grow tray.

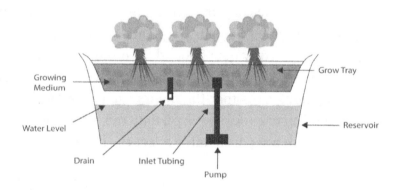

Illus. 8 – Ebb and Flow System – Stacked Container

The grow tray must fit snugly on top of the reservoir without falling into it. It needs to have a lesser depth than the reservoir, so when the tray sits on top, it leaves plenty of empty space between the bottom of the tray and the bottom of the reservoir. This empty space between them will contain the nutrient water.

Alternately, the grow tray can sit on top of the reservoir instead of nestled inside of it. Either way, grow tray and reservoir containers must work in conjunction with one another.

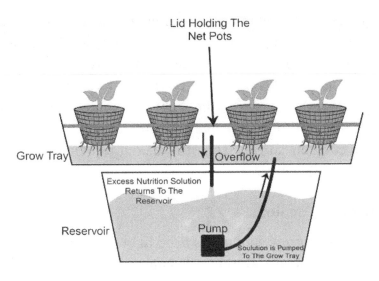

Illus. 9 - System – Reservoir Sits On Top

Another popular way to set up this system is to place the growing tray on a table and the reservoir on the floor below. Longer tubing is used to connect the two. It generally takes up more space to set it up like this. If you are setting up a large system though, the table set-up is a good option. The table will support the weight of more plants or larger plants, and it makes it easy to inspect the plants as they grow.

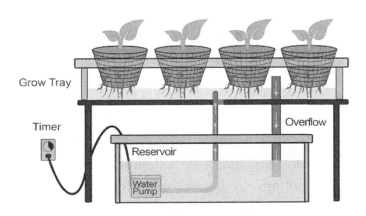

Illus. 10 – Ebb and Flow System - Grow Tray Sits On Table

An opaque reservoir container is recommended. This will make it more challenging to check the water level, but it will shield the water in the reservoir from light. If you use a transparent container, you will be able to see the water level, but you'll also need to cover the sides so the light doesn't encourage algae growth. If you opt for a transparent container, it's best to use a removable covering so you can both shield it from light and easily check the water level.

- **Growing Medium**

The grow tray or grow containers need to be filled with a medium to support the plants. Options include expanded clay pebbles (Hydroton), granulated Rockwool, vermiculite, perlite, coconut fiber, and gravel. Each medium has different absorptive capacities, so you'll need to adjust your flooding times accordingly.

A common choice is expanded clay pebbles. Clay pebbles provide great support and plant roots can easily grow through them. They are the preferred option if you place the plants directly in the grow tray instead of in individual containers. On their own, clay pebbles don't hold much water, so you'll need to flood your tray approximately every 2 hours.

Clay pebbles can be mixed 50/50 with diatomite to soak the roots for longer per flooding period. Diatomite is more absorbent than clay pebbles, so you will need fewer irrigation periods per day.

Another suggestion is a 50/50 mix of coconut fiber and perlite, with two inches of clay pebbles lining the bottom. This combination offers aeration, moisture retention, and a secure foundation for the seedlings. By lining the bottom of the tray or container with clay pebbles, you'll prevent the other medium from getting washed away when the grow tray is flooded.

Your growing medium should be allowed to dry out well in-between flooding periods. Early in the growing process, this will allow your roots to absorb plenty of oxygen and reduce the risk of root rot. Near harvest time, it will encourage your plants to flower. Plants in constantly wet medium will produce lots of green foliage instead of large fruits or vegetables.

- **Fill/Drain Overflow Fitting Kit**

These kits are readily available online or at your local home and garden store. They are inexpensive and consist of two hard plastic threaded pieces attached to a grow tray. They come in several sizes and the size of your tubing will need to match your fittings. Many companies sell inexpensive Ebb and Flow fittings sets.

The smaller piece of the kit is for the inlet. This allows water to be pumped up into the grow tray. The longer piece is for the overflow tube. It has slits around the threaded top that allow the water to flow back into the reservoir. The overflow drain is extremely important. Without it, if your pump malfunctions, water could overflow out of your grow tray.

- **Pump**

The pump should be strong enough to deliver the water from the reservoir to the grow tray but not so strong that it turns your water into a fountain. Pump specifications will indicate how high they will pump. This is measured in HEAD, so if a pump is rated at 3 feet of HEAD, then it will pump 3 feet. If the pump only has a PSI (pounds per square inch) rating, you'll need to multiply that number by 2.31 to get the HEAD. A good rule of thumb is to get a pump with a HEAD rating at least double of what you need.

- **Tubing**

The size of your tubing should match the size of your Fill/Drain fittings and your pump fitting. How much you need will depend on your system setup and the distance between your reservoir and grow tray. Clear irrigation tubing is recommended.

- **Timer**

There are two timer options: segmental (or mechanical) and digital.

A segmental timer is set to go off at specific intervals. For example, it can be set for every 20 minutes, every 6 hours, or whatever span of time you want between flooding periods. The benefits of the segmental timer over a digital one are lower costs and easier setup. The downsides are that they are less accurate than digital timers, some of them have a loud ticking noise that people find irritating, and their settings can get thrown off if you accidentally bump into them. Interruptions in power will also upset the programming. The timer shuts off when the power goes off and turns back on when the power returns, without accounting for the time it wasn't working. This can severely mess up your cycles.

With a digital timer, you can set the specific flooding time(s) each day. You can set it, for example, for every morning at 8 a.m. and every evening at 10 p.m. Digital timers are more precise than segmental ones, however, there are some downsides. They are much more expensive and can be a challenge to set up. Despite this, they have a number of advantages. Digital timers usually have a backup battery, so power outages won't interfere with the timing of your cycles. You can also set digital timers in ways that aren't possible with segmental timers. They can be set to do things on specific days of the week or combinations of days, at specific times and for very precise amounts of time. Finally, digital timers will allow you to set your flood times to smaller intervals. Given the increased reliability and greater control over irrigation times, digital timers are preferable.

A general purpose 15-amp timer is ideal. 10-amp timers often burn out so it's worth spending a few extra bucks for the 15-amp version. You'll save more cash in the long run. An indoor/outdoor timer is also recommended because they are grounded and safer to use around water.

As with anything dealing with electricity, please exercise caution when setting up your timers. It is important to avoid overloading sockets or power outputs. This can have serious consequences. Please pay close attention to the amps!

HOW TO MAKE AN EBB AND FLOW SYSTEM OUT OF PLASTIC STORAGE CONTAINERS (STACKED METHOD)

Choose a spot for your Ebb and Flow System that gets an appropriate amount of light for your growing plants. Make sure you have access to an electrical outlet. You must set it on a level surface so the water can drain through the pump efficiently. If the surface is not level, you will have water pooling at the bottom of your grow tray. Roots can rot if they are left suspended in water without enough oxygen.

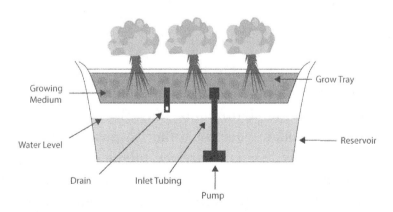

Illus. 11 – Ebb and Flow System – Stacked Container

What You Will Need:

- 16-20 gallon storage tote bin, preferably opaque or dark colored.

- 30qt clear storage tote bin, or a similar size that will fit snugly on top of the larger container

- Timer

- Clay pebbles or medium of choice

- Containers for plants (ideal size will depend on what you are growing and how many will fit in your grow tray)

- Irrigation tubing, 1/2" inner diameter, approximately 18"

- Submersible pond pump with 1/2" fittings

- Fill and drain fitting set, 1/2"

- Power drill with appropriate fittings to drill holes for fill and drain fitting set and for overflow tubing.

- Wooden dowel or flat stick longer than the height of your tallest container that you can write on.

- Nutrients

- Plants

Assembly:

- Drill two holes in the bottom of the smaller container. These are for your inlet (water going into the grow tray) and overflow (water draining out). The inlet hole will need to accommodate your fill fitting so measure accordingly. The overflow hole is where the tubing goes, so make it a little bit smaller than your tubing so it can fit securely. If you make it too big, you will need to get wider tubing.

- Attach the fill fitting set to your inlet hole.

- Cut a piece of hose to link the inlet fitting to the pump outlet. The length of tubing needs to be long enough for the pump to sit at the bottom of the reservoir while the grow tray is on top. This will take some testing; you may need to adjust it to get it right. Cut the tubing longer than you need, and then trim off small pieces until it fits nicely. You may have to secure the tubing on both sides with a zip tie. Make sure the fit is secure at both ends.

- Seat the pump at the bottom of your reservoir.

- Cut a piece of hose for your overflow. It needs to be long enough to be above your anticipated water flood height in the grow tray and still reach into the reservoir without touching the water. Fit the tubing into the overflow hole. Attach the overflow fitting to the top of the tubing so it is in the grow tray.

- Run the cord from your pump between the two stacked containers so the plug is on the outside of your system.

- Fill your reservoir 2 gallons at a time. After each addition, measure the increase in water level with a wooden dowel, marking each increment. This will let you know how much nutrient-water your plants are using and how much more you will need to add.

- Fill with a total of 10 gallons of water.

- Add the nutrients as per package instructions. Fill the plant containers with your growing medium.

- Plant the seedlings in your containers, arranging the growing medium snugly around them to keep them in place.

- Place the containers in the grow tray and fit the tray on top of the reservoir, being careful to keep the pump plug cord out.

- Set up your timer and pump. They should be set to flood 3 times a day, 15 minutes per cycle.

Caring For Your Plants In An Ebb And Flow System:

- While your plants are getting used to their new system, it is recommended that you water them from the top for a few days so the roots don't dry out.

- Inspect daily to make sure all the water is being drained properly.

- Check frequently for blockages in the overflow pipe and tubing.

- Change out nutrient-water weekly.

HOW TO SET UP A DRIP HYDROPONIC SYSTEM

The Drip System is one of the most popular design choices for hydroponic growers. It is extremely effective and uses water more efficiently than many other systems. Also, because the nutrient-water is dripped right at the plant's roots, plant growth is rapid and yields are higher.

A Drip System consists of a grow tray, a reservoir and a drip line positioned at the base of the plants. The pump is hooked up to a timer. When the pump is active, it will drip nutrient-water onto each plant. There are two types of Drip System setup, Recovery Drip System and Non-Recovery Drip System. A Recovery Drip System collects the nutrient-water runoff and recycles it back to the reservoir for reuse. A Non-Recovery Drip System does not collect or reuse the water.

The benefit of a Recovery Drip System is that you will use less water and nutrients over time. The challenge of this system is that it requires you to pay close attention to the concentration of nutrients in your water. As the water is reused, the nutrients will decrease in strength. You'll need to check pH and nutrient concentration frequently.

Non-Recovery Drip Systems are used mostly by commercial growers. The downside of this system is that it is less economical. However, growers can time watering cycles to the second. When the plants are watered, they get only as much as the growing medium can accommodate for each watering. The plants are watered more frequently and for precise amounts of time, so you can make sure the watering cycles exactly fit your plants' needs. A major benefit of this system is that you won't need to monitor the nutrient-water concentration so closely. However, you will need to change the water in the reservoir weekly to keep it from becoming stagnant or building up an excess of minerals.

Drip systems are preferable for larger plants. They provide plenty of growing medium for large root systems and you won't need huge amounts of water to flood the system. Cucumbers, tomatoes, peas, zucchini, and pumpkins are some popular choices.

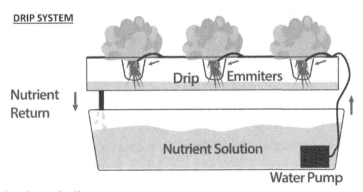

Illus. 12 – Drip System Set-Up

THE SEVEN MAIN COMPONENTS OF A DRIP SYSTEM

- Grow Containers

- Reservoir

- Growing Medium

- Tubing

- Submersible Pump

- Timer

- Drip Stakes (optional)

Grow Containers

There are many ways to set up a Drip System. The grow container you use will depend on how you choose to set it up. It's important to remember that this system doesn't already have holes in it, so you will need to make your own holes.

A common design choice is a 5-gallon bucket or several buckets connected together. Another option is potting specifically designed for a Drip System set-up, these are called Dutch Buckets or Bato Buckets and are available at most hydroponic stores.

Most growers prefer individual containers because they allow you to remove one plant without disturbing the rest. However, a single long grow tray can also be used. The benefit of using a grow tray is that it is slightly easier to set up. Instead of drilling holes in every single container, you only have to make holes in one. And, if you would like a simple, space-saving setup, you can get a grow tray that sits on top of your reservoir. This eliminates the need to find or build a table that will hold your individual containers.

For this system, it is important that your grow containers can hold a good amount of growing medium and that holes can be cut or drilled in the bottom of the buckets.

Reservoir

The reservoir in this design is very simple. It needs to hold enough nutrient enriched water to feed the plants for a week, or for however long you have decided to make your watering schedule. If you are building a recycling system, you will be conserving water and won't have to worry so much about water loss.

The reservoir can sit to the side of your grow containers or tray. If you are using a grow tray, you can situate it on top of your reservoir to conserve space. If you go down this route, keep your reservoir size in mind when purchasing your grow tray.

Medium

A few popular choices for medium are coco chips, perlite, vermiculite, clay pebbles, and rockwool. Mediums are often mixed for optimum performance. Rockwool and coco chips are highly absorbent and can lead to over-saturation if the drippers run too frequently. Clay pebbles are ideal for a Drip System because they don't absorb much nutrient-water and are unlikely to be over-saturated. When using clay pebbles it's almost impossible to over-irrigate.

Tubing

Some Drip System designs use all the same size tubing and others use different-sized tubing for the drip lines and water delivery line. In the end, system design is up to you. If you use the same diameter for both lines, you can save a few bucks on startup materials.

For large systems, it may be helpful to use larger-diameter tubing for the delivery line to reduce stress on the pump. The majority of systems use 1/2" vinyl tubing for the delivery line and 1/4" tubing for the drip lines. The size of your tubing should match your pump outlet and tube connectors.

Submersible Pump

Please see the information on pumps for Ebb and Flow Systems.

Timer

Please see information on timers for Ebb and Flow Systems.

Drip Stakes

Drip Stakes are plastic pegs that look similar to tent stakes. They attach to a drip line and carry the nutrient solution into the growing medium. The benefit of using drip stakes is that nutrients and water penetrate the medium instead of landing on top of it. This means that less nutrients will be lost through surface evaporation. It's ideal to use two stakes per plant in case one gets clogged. The downside to using drip stakes is that if they malfunction or become clogged, it's hard to notice before the plants are in trouble.

To clean your drip stakes, soak them in a bucket of vinegar solution. It's best to have backup drip stakes on hand so that when one is being cleaned, another is available to replace it. An alternative to using drip stakes is to use a ring of perforated tubing to deliver nutrient solution to your plants.

HOW TO BUILD A RECOVERY DRIP SYSTEM WITH 5-GALLON BUCKETS

Before getting started, plan out how you will arrange your buckets. The amount of T-connectors and tubing required will depend on your layout. Make sure all connectors, tubing, and fittings are the same size. The reservoir should be at least 6 inches below your buckets. A good way of setting this up is to place the buckets on a sturdy table with the reservoir beneath it. Make sure your setup is within reach of an electrical outlet.

What You Will Need:

- 4 5-gallon buckets

- 4 bulkhead fittings for your tubing

- Filter material

- Medium-sized rocks to fill the bottom ¼ of each bucket (washed and sanitized)

- Black or blue vinyl tubing

- Submersible pump

- 30-gallon storage tote bin

- Growing medium [I suggest 1 compressed block of coco chips – uncompressed, it equates to 2 cubic feet and is enough for all 4 buckets]

- 8-10 T-connectors to fit your tubing

- Timer (preferably 15 amp)

- Nutrients

- Plants

- Drill to make holes in the bottom of plastic buckets

- Paperclips and a candle or lighter

Assembly:

1. Trace the size of your bulkhead fitting onto the bottom of each of your 5-gallon buckets and cut a hole. The placement of the hole should be close to the edge of the bucket yet not so close that you will have a problem threading the fitting in it. It's ideal to make it about 1-inch from the edge.

- Be careful not to make the hole too big. If it leaks, you've got a problem. It should be just wide enough to fit the threaded end without leaving a gap.

2. Insert the fitting into the hole and tighten it. The rubber gasket should be on the outside of the bucket.

3. Cut your filter material and secure it around the fitting inside the bucket. This is to prevent growing medium or other debris from clogging up lines.

4. Fill the bottom of the buckets with the rocks.

5. Fill each bucket with the growing medium.

6. Cut a small notch in the rim of each bucket to hold the tubing securely in place.

7. On top of the growing medium, make a circle with your tubing and use the T-connectors to connect the two ends. Do this with all 4 buckets.

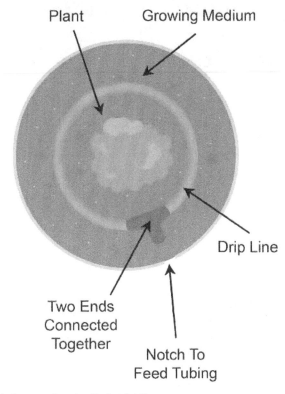

Plant   Growing Medium

Drip Line

Two Ends
Connected
Together

Notch To
Feed Tubing

Illus. 13 – Recovery Drip System – Growing Bucket Set-Up

8. Heat the end of a paperclip with a candle or lighter. Use the heated end to create holes in the drip lines. Make sure your holes face down towards the growing medium.

9. Run tubing from each bucket to the top of the reservoir.

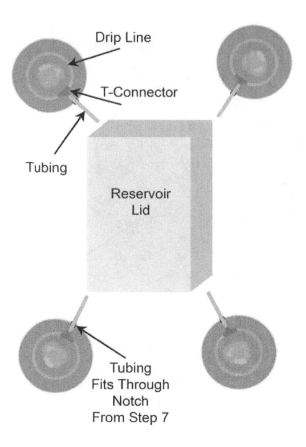

Drip Line

T-Connector

Tubing

Reservoir
Lid

Tubing
Fits Through
Notch
From Step 7

Illus. 14 – Recovery Drip System – Tubing Alignment

10. Cut a notch in the lid of your reservoir bucket large enough to fit the power cord and tubing for your pump. Cut two holes in the lid of the reservoir.

11. Place your pump in the bottom of the reservoir and arrange the power cord so it goes out through the notch.

12. Cut a length of hose to run from the pump to your bucket tubing. Attach one end to the pump. This is the feed line that delivers nutrient solution to the drip lines.

13. Run the feed line through the notch hole in the lid of your reservoir.

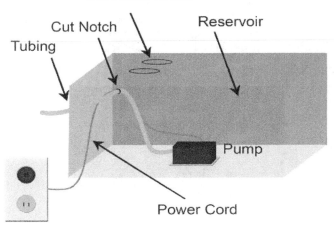

Illus. 15 – Recovery Drip System – Reservoir Set-Up

14. Attach a T-connector at the end of the feed line.

15. Cut two pieces of hose to run from either end of the T-connector.

16. Attach a T-connector to the ends of each of the hoses. You should now have 4 open connections that all feed back to the reservoir. Hose length for all steps will depend on how you have set up your buckets and how far apart they are.

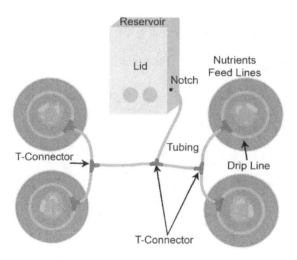

Illus. 16 – Recovery Drip System – Drip Lines Set-Up

17. Insert tubing from your buckets into each of the ends of the T-connectors.

18. Cut 4 pieces of tubing to attach to the fittings at the bottom of each bucket. With a T-connector, attach the tubing from two buckets together. Cut another length of tubing to run from this T-connector to one of the holes in the reservoir lid. This is how your nutrient-water will drain back to the reservoir. Do the same with the other two buckets, with the tubing going through a hole in the reservoir lid.

   o The exact lengths of your tubing will depend on your system setup. You will connect the bottom of 2 buckets together with tubing attached to a T-connector and then run a length of tubing from the T-connector through the hole in the reservoir lid.

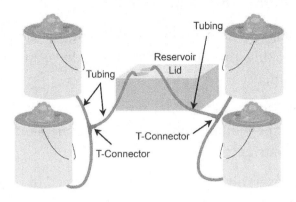

Illus. 17 – Recovery Drip System – Output Tube Set-Up

19. Set up your timer. The frequency will depend on what you're growing. A common setup is three times a day for 15 minutes each session.

20. Fill your reservoir with water and add the appropriate amount of nutrients as per package directions.

21. Plant your seedlings in the growing medium.

22. Run your system and watch your plants thrive!

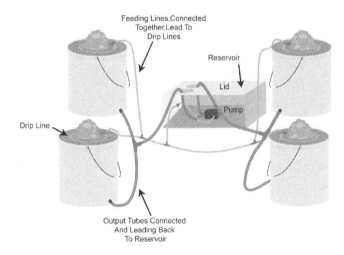

Illus. 18 – Recovery Drip System – Complete Set-Up

Caring For Your Plants In A Drip System:

- Regularly inspect the drip lines and tubing for clogs. Any material blocking the flow of water can have quick and harsh consequences.

- Check your timer and pumps on a regular basis. Any interruptions or malfunctions will cause your plants to be deprived of nutrients.

- Check your reservoir level regularly. You'll need to refill the tank more frequently if you don't recycle the water.

- Test pH and nutrient levels. If you recirculate the water, the nutrient concentration will drop before you need to change the water.

HOW TO SET UP A NUTRIENT FILM TECHNIQUE SYSTEM

Nutrient Film Systems work with gravity to send a thin film of nutrient solution continuously flowing over the exposed plant roots. The benefit of this technique is that the plants receive a constant flow of nutrients. The downside is that any disruption in the system, for even the smallest amount of time, can cause catastrophic failure for the entire crop.

In an NFT System, nutrient-enriched water is pumped from the reservoir through tubing to the gullies or channels which hold the plants. The water flows down the sloped sides of the channels, wetting the plant's roots. The plants are suspended above the water at the top of the channels with the roots hanging down. The shallow film of nutrient-water flows by and feeds the roots. It then drains down another tube where it is fed back to the reservoir for re-circulation.

The NFT system provides nutrient solution to the roots without flooding them. The exposed root tops also receive oxygen, providing your plants with optimal conditions for fast and healthy growth. This system doesn't require the extensive setup and monitoring required by most other systems. As the water flows continuously, there's no need to worry about specific time schedules.

The only upkeep this system requires is a weekly change-out of the nutrient solution. Plus, you'll need little to no growing medium. You can set this system up vertically or horizontally. The ideal arrangement will depend on the plants you wish to grow. It's also relatively easy to add additional channels to your system if you'd like to expand it. NFT systems are preferable for short-season crops like lettuce and herbs.

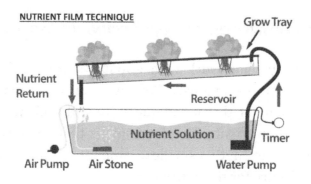

Illus. 19 – Nutrient Film Technique Set-Up

THE FIVE MAIN COMPONENTS OF AN NFT SYSTEM

- Reservoir

- Grow Tubes (also called Gullies or Channels)

- Growing Baskets, Medium, or Starter Cubes

- Submersible Pump

- Tubing

- **Reservoir**

The size of your reservoir is dependent on the size of your system. Too small a reservoir will create instability in your nutrient solution.

- For small plants, supply a minimum of a ½ gallon of water per plant

- For medium plants, supply a minimum of 1 ½ gallons of water per plant

- For large plants, supply a minimum of 2 ½ gallons of water, per plant

The reservoir should be placed below the channels to ensure the pump operates effectively.

- **Grow Tubes (a.k.a. Channels or Gullies)**

PVC, stainless steel, and rain guttering are common material choices for the channels. Wood channels can also work if they are lined with waterproof plastic. Avoid using heavy metals.

PVC is often used because it's inexpensive and easy to set up. The downside of PVC is its roundness, which can cause the nutrient-water to flow unevenly around the plant's roots. This is mainly a problem with larger plants. Flat channels will ensure effective water flow and prevent uneven root growth. There are also a number of hydroponic companies that make channels specifically for this system.

The width of your channel should be set to the size needed to accommodate the root systems of mature plants. Quick-growing plants like lettuce only need about four inches in width. Slightly larger plants like strawberries will need about six inches. Larger, longer-term plants such as tomatoes need approximately eight inches.

The channel should be covered to prevent sunlight from contacting the plant's roots. Removable covers are best because they will allow you to inspect the roots and check for blockages in the system.

- **Flow Rate and Channel Slope**

When determining where to set up your channels and slope, take ceiling height into account and make sure there is adequate space for the plants to grow. The slope of the channel determines how fast the water will flow through the system. The recommended slope is a 1:30 or 1:40 ratio. This means that you will want a one inch drop for every 30 or 40 inches of horizontal length. The maximum channel length for this slope is 40 feet. If the slope is flatter, recommended channel length is 20 feet.

For small, quick-growing plants like herbs and lettuce, a flow rate of 5-1 liter per minute is recommended. For larger plants such as tomatoes, a flow rate of 2 liters per minute is recommended.

It's best to set your system up so that you can adjust the slope depending on your plants' needs. This will also allow you to clear the channel if roots grow to block the system.

The channels should be as straight as possible. Any sag or give in the material will cause water to pool and reduce the efficiency of the system.

Plants near the end of the channel will get less nutrients. For larger channels, you'll need to install a second reservoir to make sure all plants get enough nutrients.

- **Growing Baskets, Medium, or Starter Cubes**

Net pots or other types of growing baskets can be set into the top or the cover of the channel. Holes must be cut for each basket. It's important to remember that the baskets should not touch the water. The roots need to dangle in the air with just the tips touching the water solution. If the roots need support while they are young, use clay pebbles as a growing medium to secure them. As the roots grow out, you will likely find that a growing medium becomes unnecessary.

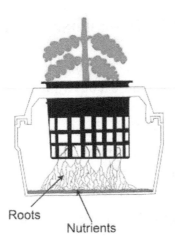

Roots

Nutrients

Illus. 20 – Net Pot, Roots and Nutrients

Starter cubes are excellent for this system and easy to use. You can start your seeds in the cube and transfer the entire cube into the NFT system when it's ready. Many NFT System growers use the starter cubes without a net pot or basket because the mass of roots is strong enough to support itself. Home and garden stores carry a wide variety of starter cubes.

Submersible Pump

Please see section on pumps for Ebb and Flow Systems.

Tubing

Please see the section on tubing for Ebb and Flow Systems.

How to Build an NFT Hydroponic System with PVC Pipes

This design requires a drawn-out plan before you begin. The design will depend on where you want to place it and what you intend to grow. It can be hung from a ceiling, propped up on wooden stands, or placed on a table with a built-in slope. As this system is gravity-driven, the most important thing is the flow. One end of the channel must be higher than the other. But not too high! This particular design needs approximately 1" of a slope per 30-40" of horizontal length, depending on what you are growing.

Before you build this hydroponic system, decide where you will place it, what plants you will grow, and how you will give it the desired slope. Building the slope can be as simple as placing the system on a table and propping up one end with wedges. This system requires the use of a pump, so make sure your system is within reach of an electrical outlet.

What You Will Need:

- 4" PVC Pipe, 30" length
- 2 adjustable rubber end-caps for PVC with hose clamps
- Net pots or other grow containers
- Submersible pump
- Irrigation tubing (make sure it will fit the output of your pump)
- Plumbing cement
- Growing medium
- Plants
- Nutrients
- Reservoir container (20+ gallon size)

- Drill

- Hole Saw

- Tape measure

- Zip Ties, wire shelf hangers, assorted lumber to make a stand, or wooden wedges to make the necessary slope

Assembly:

1. Cut holes in the top of your PVC pipe for your net pots or growing containers. The number of holes you will need and their size will depend on what you're growing. Also, the distance between each plant/hole is important. If you would like 3" between each plant, measure 3" from one end of the PVC pipe. Cut out a circle that will fit your grow container. Measure another 3" and repeat until you get to the end of the PVC. [Make sure pots are NOT going to fall through the holes!]

2. Attach adjustable rubber caps to the ends of the PVC pipe.

3. Cut another hole in the top of the PVC to fit your tubing. This is where nutrient solution will be pumped in from the reservoir. Make sure the hole is the same size or a little smaller than your tubing so it fits snug.

4. On the opposite end of your PVC pipe cut a hole in the bottom to fit your tubing. This will drain the water to the reservoir. Make sure it is placed beyond where the roots will sit. You don't want it to drain before it reaches the last of your plants

PVC Pipe W/hole For Pots
Side View

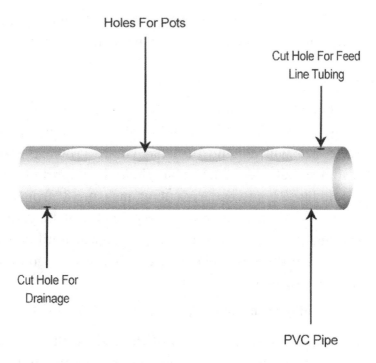

Holes For Pots

Cut Hole For Feed
Line Tubing

Cut Hole For
Drainage

PVC Pipe

Illus. 21 – NFT System – PVC Pipe with Holes for Net Pots

5. Using the flow rate calculation discussed earlier, determine the ideal slope for your system.

6. You can use wire or zip ties to attach your PVC pipe to the ceiling of your room. Alternately, you can build a wooden stand with a slight incline, or place the system on a table and use wooden wedges to create the desired slope.

7. Cut two holes in the lid of the reservoir to fit your irrigation tubing. One is for output and the other for input.

8. Place the water pump in the bottom of the reservoir.

9. Attach the irrigation hose to the pump. Use plumbing cement if necessary to secure all seals. Feed the irrigation hose through one of the holes in your reservoir lid and lead it to the hole in your PVC pipe.

10. Connect another length of tubing from the hole in the bottom of the PVC pipe to the second hole in the lid of your reservoir. Use plumbing cement to secure the seal if necessary.

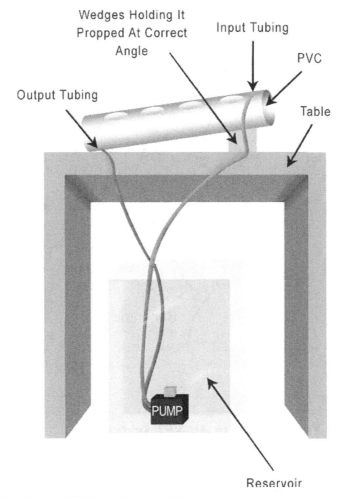

Illus. 22 – NFT System – PVC Pipe and Reservoir Set-Up

11. Fill your reservoir with water and nutrients as per package instructions.

12. Fill the growing containers with growing medium and plants and place them in the holes in the PVC.

13. Turn on your pump and test the system for leaks and slope/flow rate. Make sure the roots touch the flowing water.

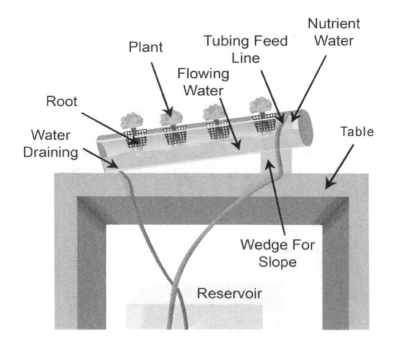

Illus. 23 – NFT System – Plant and Nutrient Water Set-Up

Caring For Your Plants In An NFT System:

- Check the pH often and adjust as needed.

- Inspect the pump regularly.

- Keep an eye on root growth. Make sure the roots don't block the channel.

- Inspect the tubing for blockages.

- Change out the nutrient solution weekly.

How to Set Up an Aeroponic Hydroponic System

The Aeroponic System is the most technical of the hydroponic systems. However, it's still easy for the home gardener to build. In an Aeroponic System, the plant's roots hang in mid-air in an enclosed system. They are regularly misted with nutrient solution. This way, the roots receive plenty of oxygen and other nutrients to maximize plant growth. Since the roots receive so much oxygen, the plants will grow more quickly with this system than with the others described above.

The main advantages of Aeroponic Systems are that they use minimal, if any, growing medium and less water than any other system.

The downside is that these systems are more expensive to build than others. Plus, the roots are susceptible to drying out since they are continuously exposed to the air. Any disruption in the irrigation system could destroy the entire crop. The sprinkler heads tend to clog so it is important to have spares on hand. It isn't a good idea to disrupt the water supply to the plants while cleaning the clogged heads. Instead, you can switch out the heads that are clogged so you can fix them without having to rush.

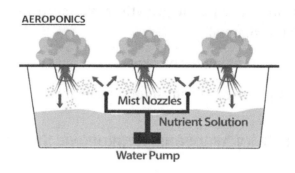

Illus. 24 – Aeroponics Set-Up

There are two types of Aeroponic system: Low-Pressure and High-Pressure. Most often when people talk about Aeroponic Systems, they're talking about the Low-Pressure variety. However, High-Pressure systems have distinct advantages. The main difference between the Low-Pressure and High-Pressure systems is the size of the water droplets. While this might seem like a small thing, it can mean a lot to your plants.

Low-Pressure Systems have larger water droplets. High-Pressure Systems, often called "true Aeroponics", employ very fine water droplets. With fine water droplets, the roots will be misted with nutrient solution. The plants receive more oxygen because they aren't being drenched by the nutrient solution. High-Pressure Systems are more complex and expensive to build than Low-Pressure Systems. However, if you can set one up, it will pay dividends in your plant growth.

Due to the relative ease in construction, this guide focuses primarily on Low-Pressure Hydroponics Systems.

- Enclosed Grow Chamber

- Net Pots (or other containers for plants)

- Misting/Sprinkler Heads

- Submersible Pump

- Reservoir

- Tubing

- Timer

Enclosed Grow Chamber

The grow chamber needs to be airtight and opaque so no light gets in. A large opaque tote bin will serve well for this purpose. Make sure it's tall enough for your roots to hang down without touching the bottom. Also, if your reservoir is directly below, make sure the roots won't touch the water.

Net Pots/Plant Containers

Please refer to the section on Net Pots for the Water Culture System.

Misting/Sprinkler Heads

The spray from your misting heads should overlap. When planning your design, keep this in mind. Make sure your setup ensures that all roots will be covered by the spray.

Misting heads are available from garden stores and online. There are many different types and sizes to choose from. It's best to look at reviews and read what other growers have used to find the best one for your situation. The ideal solution for you will depend on what you're growing and how you have designed the system.

Submersible Pump

Please refer to the section on <u>pumps for Ebb and Flow Systems.</u> With each added misting head, water pressure will drop. Keep this in mind when selecting a pump. This system needs a high HEAD rating.

Reservoir

Please see refer to the section on <u>reservoirs for Ebb and Flow Systems.</u> For the most simple setups, the reservoir and the grow chamber are the same size. However, different designs may require larger reservoirs.

Tubing

Please refer to the section on <u>tubing for the Ebb and Flow System.</u>

Timer

Please refer to the section on <u>timers for the Ebb and Flow System.</u>

HOW TO BUILD A 5-GALLON BUCKET LOW-PRESSURE AEROPONIC SYSTEM

This system can also be easily adapted for a large storage bin. Instead of one sprinkler though, there will be several connected with PVC pipe. You'll need a pump and timer, so place the bucket near an electrical outlet

What You Will Need:

- 1 5-gallon bucket with lid
- Net pots (the size will depend on what you are growing)
- Timer
- Pump

- 1 360-degree sprinkler head with 1/2" thread

- 1/2" x 12" threaded poly riser

- Hole saw

- Drill

- Regular saw

Assembly:

1. Cut holes in the lid of the bucket to fit your net pots. Space them out evenly. Make sure pots will not fall all the way through but will fit snugly.

2. Screw the threaded poly riser into the pump. Cut it to the desired height.

3. Attach the sprinkler head to the top of the poly riser. The height of both riser and sprinkler head should be lower than the expected length of the roots.

4. Place the pump with attached riser and sprinkler head onto the bottom of the bucket.

5. Lead the cord for the pump out through one of the holes in the lid and attach it to the timer.

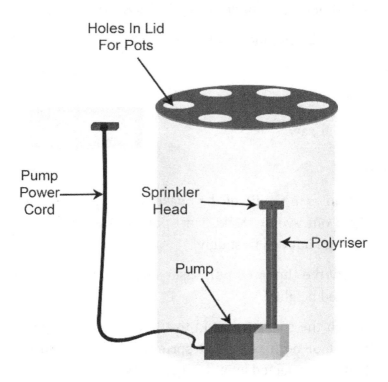

Holes In Lid
For Pots

Pump
Power
Cord

Sprinkler
Head

Polyriser

Pump

Illus. 25 – 5-Gallon Bucket Aeroponic Set-Up

6. Fill the bucket with 2 gallons of water and the appropriate amount of nutrients as per package directions.

7. Secure the lid on top of the bucket. Arrange the plants in the net pots. Clay pebbles can be used to keep them in place if necessary.

8. Turn the pump on.

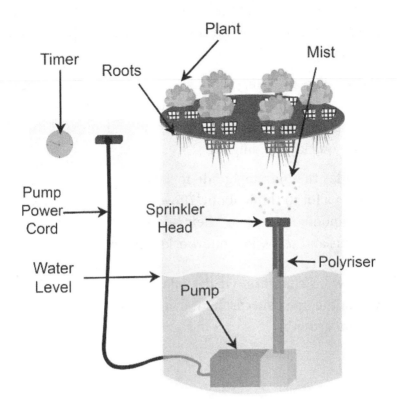

Illus. 26 – 5-Gallon Bucket Aeroponics – Plants and Nutrient Water Set-Up

Caring For Your Plants in An Aeroponic System:

- Pay close attention to the temperature in your grow space. It's all too easy to cook the exposed roots of your plants. Grow lights can exacerbate the problem if you're not careful. It may be necessary to invest in an air conditioner or use more efficient lights. Between spray cycles, the roots will be exposed and fragile. Treat them carefully!

- The reservoir temperature should be kept at 64F or slightly below. If the water is too hot, it will burn the roots.

- Clean filters, pumps, and tubing regularly. The biggest rookie mistake is to allow clogged nozzles to go unnoticed. This can endanger plant growth, from one plant to the entire crop. Thankfully, this is completely preventable if you keep a close eye on the system and keep fresh nozzles to hand.

- In this system, everything happens faster. The plants grow quicker, which is great. The other side of this, though, is that problems will develop faster and impact the plants more quickly. Be diligent.

This concludes the building guide for all six hydroponic systems. I know there's a lot to think about. However, one of the great things about hydroponic systems is their adaptability. Try out a few of these systems and see which one works best for you.

In the following chapters, we'll explore the pro tips for making your system the most successful it can be and achieving maximum healthy plant growth.

CHAPTER 2: GROWING MEDIUMS, NUTRIENTS & LIGHTING

I n nature, plants rely upon soil for stability and nutrients. Since hydroponic systems use no soil, the plants need to be stabilized and obtain nutrients in other ways. This chapter will help you determine which growing medium is best for your system. We'll also address different nutrient choices and lighting methods. Mediums, nutrients, and lighting are vitally important for the health of your plants.

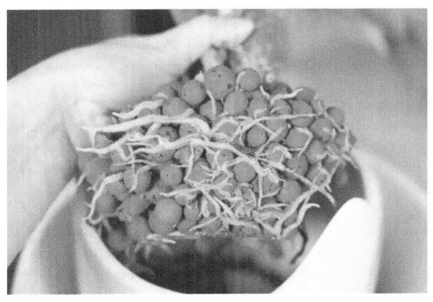

Firn/Shutterstock.com

With regard to medium, growers have plenty of options. Many people end up using a mix of different mediums. The ideal mix depends on availability in your area. Nutrients are produced by several different commercial companies, and each has pros and cons. Once you understand how to interpret the numbers on the bottle, you'll be much better prepared to decide which is best for your system. Lighting is pretty straight-forward. If your system has access to the sun, then you won't need to consider lighting at all. On the other hand, appropriate lighting is a necessity for indoor growing.

GROWING MEDIUMS

As mentioned before, you have many choices when it comes to growing mediums. The ideal medium for your system depends on which hydroponic system you are using and what you are growing. Common growing mediums are rockwool, coco coir, peat moss, clay pellets, perlite, vermiculite, and gravel.

ROCKWOOL

Rockwool comes in slabs, blocks, and loose fill. It is an inorganic substance, made by melting rocks and spinning them into long, fine fibers. In this sense, it is similar to fiberglass.

Rockwool blocks are great for starting seedlings. In many systems, you don't even have to remove the seedlings from the Rockwool to add them to your system. Simply transfer the entire block with plant to your grow pot.

Rockwool naturally has a high pH level. Because of this, it is necessary to soak it before use. It's also difficult to dispose of properly as the thin fibers won't biodegrade. In essence, they'll last forever.

The high-absorbency of Rockwool makes it a great choice for the Drip System. However, it can become over-saturated so you'll need to monitor the system carefully.

COCO COIR

Coco coir is made of ground coconut husks. It is quickly becoming a popular choice amongst hydroponic growers. In nature, coconut husks protect coconuts from sun, sea, and salt damage. When the coconut is ready to sprout, the husk will act as a natural growing medium. By using ground coconut husks in your hydroponic garden, you'll provide these same advantages for your own plants. Coco coir is a renewable, sustainable material. It also looks very much like soil, making it appealing to those who prefer a more natural approach.

Coco coir can hold up to ten times its weight in water. This is great for a hydroponic system. At the same time, it can cause your system to retain too much water. Because of this, Coco Coir is not recommended for constant-flow systems.

Coco coir comes in compressed dry bricks that need to be rehydrated before use. This adds a little extra work to the hydroponic process, but it's not difficult and won't take much time.

If you use coco coir, it's important to choose a nutrient mix specifically designed for this medium. Coco coir binds with iron and magnesium and can starve your plants of these essential elements.

This medium works wonderfully when mixed 50/50 with perlite. Coco Coir retains nutrient solution, while perlite retains oxygen.

EXPANDED CLAY PELLETS

Also referred to as Hydroton, clay pellets are great for many reasons. The clay pellets expand in water to make round, porous balls. Their round shape is stable enough to hold a seedling in place without denying it oxygen or water. These elements can still flow freely around the plant's roots.

One thing to consider is that clay pellets are heavy compared to most mediums. If you fill an entire grow tray with them, you may have a weight issue. Plus, the pellets can dry out quickly because there is so much space between them. If you're not careful, this can cause your roots to dry out, stopping plant growth altogether.

Clay pellets are great for a Drip System because you can run the dripper constantly without worrying about over-saturation or excess dryness.

PERLITE

Perlite is aerated volcanic rock. It is light and porous and has been used for years in both soil and hydroponic gardens. Perlite is excellent for retaining oxygen levels. The downside is that it is light in weight. It can easily get washed away or shifted from where you want it. For this reason, it is commonly mixed with another medium, like coco coir or vermiculite.

VERMICULITE

Vermiculite is a mineral that expands when heated and forms a pebble shape. It holds water and wicks well, meaning it will draw water and nutrients upwards. The downsides are that it can hold too much water and it is more expensive than most other mediums. If you choose to include vermiculite in your mix, the best option is to blend a small amount of it with other mediums.

GRAVEL

Gravel is the cheapest material you can use. If you're on a tight budget, this is the material for you. You'll need to wash it before you use it, to protect the sensitive roots of your plants from any harmful bacteria or other detrimental substances that may be present. Another downside is that it's quite heavy. If you use lots of gravel, you'll need to make sure your system has enough structural stability to handle it.

STARTER PLUGS/CUBES

Starter plugs are small, compact masses of material used to start seedlings. There is a hole in the top of the plug for the seed to be placed. Once they are watered, seeds will germinate in starter plugs faster than in soil or other materials. They contain all the nutrients that your seeds need to get started. Some starter plugs even come with seeds already in them.

Starter plugs can be made of a number of different materials. The most common materials are Rockwool, peat moss, and pine pulp. If they dry out, it can be hard to rehydrate them, so make sure to keep them sufficiently watered.

The biggest benefit of starter plugs in a hydroponic system is that the seedlings don't need to be transplanted. They can be placed directly into your system without being removed from the plug.

Growing Medium Notes

Please note that I do not include peat moss in this list. Even though it has been commonly used in hydroponic systems, it is not a renewable resource. If you'd like to learn more about this, do a little digging. There's plenty of available information which explains in-depth the environmental impact of extensive peat moss use.

Note: The information on nutrients and lighting is similar to the information provided in the first book. You can

either refresh your knowledge or jump directly to the next chapter.

NUTRIENTS

Since hydroponic systems don't use soil, the nutrients added to the water must contain all the minerals plants need to thrive. The selection of the appropriate nutrient solution is one of the most important decisions of your hydroponic plan. Healthy plant growth depends on having the right balance of nutrients.

There are 16 essential elements that plants need. These elements are absorbed by the plant in different ways. Some are transferred to the plant through the roots, while others are taken in through the pores of the leaf. Carbon, Oxygen, and Hydrogen, three of the most necessary elements, can be obtained from both air and water. These need to be monitored and balanced. One common problem in hydroponics is a lack of sufficient carbon dioxide.

The next big three elements, Nitrogen, Phosphorus, and Potassium, are provided in the fertilizer nutrient blends made for growing hydroponic plants. A fine balance of these is extremely important. This is often referred to as the N-P-K mix. When looking at bottles or bags of fertilizer, you'll see a list of three numbers on the front, separated by dashes. It will look something like this: 3-4-1. These three numbers refer to the Nitrogen, Phosphorus, and Potassium (N-P-K) proportion of the mix.

Calcium, Magnesium, and Sulfur are the next most essential elements. They are also supplied by fertilizer supplements. Calcium is provided through a calcium nitrate ($CaNO_3$) fertilizer. Magnesium and Sulfur are available with magnesium sulfate ($MgSO_4$) supplements.

The remaining 7 essential elements, Copper, Zinc, Boron, Molybdenum, Iron, Manganese, and Chlorine, are rarely deficient. If there is an Iron deficiency, you can supplement your plants with chelated iron.

To make sure your plants get everything they need, specially crafted fertilizer mixes are made for hydroponic crops. These mixes can be added to the water in your reservoir and distributed to your plants through the hydroponic system. Specific fertilizers are created for specific crops. They're not all interchangeable. The hydroponic nutrient mix for tomatoes will be quite different from the one for lettuce.

Nutrient mixes are available as liquid or granules. Liquid fertilizer is easy to use. You just pour it into the water reservoir as per the bottle's instructions. The downside to using liquid fertilizer is that it is more expensive and bulkier to store. Granulated fertilizer is more cost effective, easier to store, and often comes in bulk. However, it isn't as easy to use because it has to be mixed prior to use and it doesn't always dissolve completely. Either one will work fine, so it's a matter of personal preference and what's required by your particular system.

Granulated mixes are available in three types. The one-part mixes are simple and straight-forward. The fertilizer is mixed as indicated on the bag. These are simple to use, but not the best for making stock solutions. Some nutrients in high concentration will form solids. A multi-part solution is better for making stock solutions because the compounds are kept separately. They are relatively easy to mix, too. This is the most common choice for growers who are using granulated nutrient mixes. However, the multi-part mixes can be expensive, so it isn't the best choice unless you have a very large garden operation.

Hydroponic fertilizer mixes are also specialized for different stages of growth. They will indicate on the package the stage of growth for which they are designed. Examples of growth stages include vegetative (leaf growth) or blooming (flowering). You'll want to know what you actually want from the plant. Spinach, lettuce, and kale, for example, will benefit most from vegetative growth because you harvest the leaves of the plant. For plants that deliver a fruit or flower, you'll want to use the vegetative mix up to the point where you want them to flower. Then, switch to the flowering mix.

Nutrients are further classified based on the growing medium that is being used. The majority of nutrient mixes are made for a specific growing medium. Pay attention to package specifics and do your homework. If you're using a vermiculite mix but your growth medium is clay pellets, then you won't get optimal results. If the package doesn't give you all the details you need, then a simple online search will lead you in the right direction.

Hydroponic nutrients can be organic or synthetic. Organic fertilizers are best for systems that recirculate or reuse the nutrient solution. These mixes often include materials that can clog up sprayers, drip lines, and pumps. Synthetic nutrients don't have this issue and are therefore more commonly used in hydroponic systems. Organic fertilizers will often have a lower N-P-K listing than synthetic. However, this doesn't mean they are of a lower quality. Synthetic mixes are generally fast-release, as opposed to the slow-release of organic, and so the readily available N-P-K is higher in the synthetic. However, organic mixes will deliver a natural, time release fertilizer that won't burn your roots.

NUTRIENTS YOU NEED FOR YOUR HYDROPONIC SYSTEM

- An N-P-K mix, formulated for the crop you are growing

- Calcium Nitrate (CaNO3)

- Magnesium Sulfate (MgSO4)

HOW TO ADD NUTRIENTS TO YOUR HYDROPONIC SYSTEM

1. Mix the solution as per the package instructions and add it to your reservoir.

2. Check your pH balance on a daily or weekly basis. (This timing will depend on the system you are using and the crops you are growing.)

3. Change out or top off your solution weekly or bi-weekly. (Again, the timing depends on the system and crops).

4. Flush your crop before harvesting. (Flushing your hydroponic crop means allowing it to grow without nutrient solution for a brief period prior to harvesting.)

TESTING THE PH

pH is the balance of acidity and alkalinity of your water. The nutrients you add to your water will influence the acid/alkaline balance. pH is measured on a scale from 0-14, with 0 being the most acidic and 14 being the most alkaline or basic. pH tests will tell you how well the plants will be able to use the nutrients. Each plant prefers a specific pH balance, and your plants won't be able to absorb the needed nutrients if the pH is too high or too low. Measure the pH after you've added the nutrients and then adjust as needed. A good baseline is to keep it between 5.5 and 6.5.

pH testing devices include paper litmus test strips, liquid test kits, and electronic testing pens. Paper test strips are the cheapest way to go, but they lack accuracy. Litmus strips change color when you dip them in solution. The resultant color reflects the pH. But checking the resulting color against the chart is a bit subjective, so you won't be able to determine the acidity of the solution with any amount of precision. The results can also be skewed if your nutrient solution isn't clear, which is a problem because many nutrient solutions will color the water.

Liquid test kits offer a fair balance of cost and precision. To use a liquid test kit, you take a small sample of solution and place it into a vial which contains a pH-sensitive dye. As with the litmus test, you will compare the resulting color with a chart. This will help you to determine the pH balance of your solution. The color changes are easier to see, and the test is a bit more sensitive than a litmus test, so the liquid test kit is somewhat more accurate. However, liquid test kits can also be skewed by the color of your solution (if it's not clear), so they aren't 100% accurate. However, unless your plants are extremely sensitive, liquid test kits are accurate enough.

If your number one consideration is accuracy in pH testing, digital meters are the way to go. They are more expensive, but they will tell you the pH to a tenth, and they won't be skewed by the color of your nutrient solution. To use a digital meter, you just insert the tip of the meter in the solution and it will provide you with a digital reading. The one thing you have to watch out for with these meters is calibration. To calibrate them, you must dip them in a pH neutral solution to provide a baseline. This is easier than it sounds, and you can find plenty of information about it online if you need.

If you need to adjust the pH, phosphoric acid will raise acidity (lower pH) and lemon juice will lower acidity (raise pH). There are also a number of pH adjustment products readily available in hydroponic stores.

FLUSHING

The nutrients you feed your plants build up in them and can cause bitter or chemical tastes. Flushing out the plants before harvesting

144

ensures a good end product. Do this for 4-7 days prior to the harvest. The most traditional way to do this is to irrigate your plants with pure water and allow them to process it through their system for up to a week before harvesting. If you'd like to get fancy, several flushing agents are readily available at hydroponic stores. They'll speed up the process and ensure a complete flush. Remember – flushing is extremely important. You'll be able to taste the difference, regardless of what it is you're growing.

OPTIONAL ADDITIVES FOR THE PLANTS

Bloom Maximizers

These are added to your nutrient solution to increase the size and yield of your plants. They are usually high in Phosphorus and Potassium. This additive can be quite expensive, but it's generally worth the price for the boost it gives the plants. Nutrient burn can be a problem when using this so monitor the plants closely if you choose to use it. (Nutrient burn is the plant's equivalent of chemical burn. If you see the roots turn a different color, take on an unhealthy texture, or shrivel after adding the solution, flush the reservoir with pure water so that the plants can recover. It's far better, though, to make sure that you use the right concentration and you don't have to resort to damage control.) Bloom maximizers should only be used during the flowering stage of growth.

Mycorrhizae and Other Fungi

Mycorrhizae are small fungal filaments that penetrate the roots, increasing their surface area. They also gather and break down certain nutrients. Mycorrhizae exist in a symbiotic relationship with nearly all plant species. They help plants to absorb nutrients and water. In return, they receive some of the sugars that plants create through photosynthesis.

Mycorrhizal fungi can be added directly to the nutrient solution and will grow alongside the roots as they do in nature. You can also add other fungi such as Trichoderma to aid in breaking down nutrients and making your crops more resistant to soil pests. Trichoderma and Mycorrhizal fungi are readily available in hydroponics stores. They will help your plants to remain healthy and grow more quickly.

Vitamins and Enzymes

Thiamine (vitamin B-1) supports and strengthens the immune system of plants so they can better withstand stress and disease. It also facilitates root development, making the plants more resistant to shock and helping them to take in nutrients more quickly. This is especially important when transplanting. Enzymes break down nutrients, making them easier for plants to absorb. They are also helpful for preventing algae growth.

Root Stimulators

Root stimulators are compounds that replicate the benefits of natural soil. There are beneficial microbes in soil that promote plant growth, just as there are harmful microbes that interfere with plant growth. Rooting stimulators introduce the healthy microbes into your hydroponics system, helping your plants to have stronger immune systems, more access to nitrogen, and faster root development. They are also excellent at preventing bacterial complications in the root structure.

Overall, root stimulators promote fast, healthy plant growth. If you add root stimulators at the beginning of your growing cycle, they will continue to reproduce throughout your plants growth from seedling to harvest, providing more robust, faster-growing crops from the start.

Nutrient Notes:

When searching for nutrients, you will encounter a slew of brands and products. While they'll all claim to be the best, there's a great deal of variety in quality from one brand to the next, even among products designed for the same purpose. A brand or company might be good for one thing, but not so great for another.

The best way to deal with this is to read reviews from several growers to find out which products they prefer. This will provide you with solid feedback from people who have been there. Find hydroponic forums where you can post the details of your system and crop. You'll get plenty of responses from experienced growers that will direct you to products that have worked for them in similar situations.

Water quality is of utmost importance in a hydroponic system. Do not underestimate the necessity of good clean water. Distilled or RO (reverse osmosis) water is the best choice. Tap water or city water can have pollutants, chemicals, additives, and any number of things that can potentially have a negative impact on plant growth. This being said, plants use *lots* of water. If your prime concern is economy, then you'll use what you've got. Just remember that you get out of the plant what you put into it.

LIGHTING

Plants needs around twelve hours of light per day. Of course, this will vary depending on the plant that you are growing. Some plants prefer a great deal of light, while others do quite well with only a moderate amount. Remember that plants get their energy from light. If your hydroponic system isn't in a place where it is getting natural light from the sun, you'll need to set up a lighting system.

Plants have rhythms, just like we do. Look into the preferred light cycles of your plants, and set up timers so that you give them a schedule as close as possible to their natural cycle. The optimal light schedule will differ depending on the growth stage of the plant as well. Many plants grow well vegetatively when provided with constant light, but need cycles of light and darkness to trigger flowering.

Maciej/Shutterstock.com

The type of lighting you need depends on a wide variety of factors specific to your system: enclosure type, plant type, system size, ventilation, and last but not least, budget. Fluorescent tubes are good for a single low-budget system. Small systems will fare better with CFLs (Compact Fluorescent Lamps). These lights were designed as an efficient alternative to incandescent bulbs. They screw into a standard socket and provide sufficient light, but you may want to arrange reflectors so that the light is focused on the plant.

HIDs (High Intensity Discharge lamps) are another option. They are a bit more costly than CFLs, but they are a preferred lighting option for experienced growers. This is because they have a very high light output and are four to eight times more efficient than standard incandescent bulbs. However, they produce a lot of heat, so you'll have to ventilate your system to prevent it from drying out.

Another option is to use LEDs (Light Emitting Diode lamps). This is the high-tech option and will cost quite a bit more at the beginning, but they use a fraction of the electricity of other options and produce less heat. LEDs can also be calibrated to produce the exact spectrum of light that your plant needs. If you only plan to grow one crop, it's probably not worth it to purchase LEDs. But, if this is the beginning of a long relationship with hydroponic growing, they will more than pay off in the long run.

FLUORESCENT LIGHTS

Fluorescent lights are available in a wide range of sizes and spectrums. They are not ideal for large plants but they will work. They are generally inexpensive, easy to set up, and will work in a pinch.

COMPACT FLUORESCENT BULBS

These are a good choice because they aren't too expensive and they don't require any special wiring or set-up (they screw into a regular light socket). They produce light in all directions and are best used with a reflector so you don't waste any heat or light.

HIGH-INTENSITY DISCHARGE (HID) LIGHTS

HID lights have a high light output and are a preferred choice for growers. Using HIDs will be better for your plants than fluorescents and less expensive than incandescent bulbs in the long run. At the same time, they are expensive, require a special set-up, and need ventilation because of their high heat output.

LED LIGHTS

LED lights can provide the exact spectrum of light your plant needs. They last longer than all other lights and use less electricity. The upfront cost, however, is imposing. As mentioned above, LEDs are worth it if you plant to be growing many crops over the years. For a one-off, though, you may be better off with a different option.

Chapter 3: How to Maintain a Hydroponic System

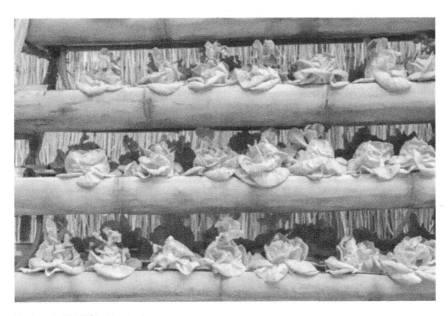

Feelphoto2521/Shutterstock.com

A s with any garden venture, your hydroponic system will require maintenance to keep your plants healthy and your system operating well. You won't have to weed plants beds or mess with soil. Instead, you'll have to keep a close eye on a number of factors: temperature, water level, nutrient level, and cleanliness. Maintaining each of these factors is vital to the healthy growth of your crop. Monitor your system on a regular basis to make sure everything is working properly.

CLEANLINESS

Clean the grow space before you set up your system. Clean your grow boxes, reservoirs, grow pots and any other equipment you are using. This is best done with a 10% bleach solution.

Any leaves, flowers, or organic matter that falls off your plants should be cleared away immediately. Don't leave it lying around. This will encourage pests and diseases to take hold, as they thrive on dead plant matter.

NUTRIENT SOLUTION

It is recommended that you completely change out the nutrient water solution in your reservoir weekly. In some cases, it's okay to just top up the water. However, if you have an imbalance of micronutrients or a disease is trying to take hold, a top-up won't prevent it.

WATERING

"How much water do I need to use?" This is the most common question asked by new hydroponic growers and the most difficult to answer. The answer is completely dependent on what kind of system you have, what plants you are growing, the growing medium, surrounding temperature, etc. Here's the rule of thumb: Water enough to keep the roots wet, but not so much that they remain saturated.

If you notice the growing medium and roots getting dry between watering cycles, increase the irrigation frequency. If they seem to be wet all the time, decrease the frequency. The frequency can be adjusted as many times as you need until you have it correct for your system. Remember that as your plants grow, their water needs will change.

In general, there is no need to water at night. Plants absorb the most water when it is light outside. They don't use much during the dark hours. When you set up your timer, plan the irrigation cycles for the daylight hours. If you notice that your plants are getting dry at night, add a nighttime watering cycle as well.

RESERVOIR TEMPERATURE

The temperature of the water in your reservoir should be around 70F. If you struggle to maintain this temperature, consider getting a heating mat and placing it below the reservoir. Alternately, you can put a heating element inside the reservoir. If you have a small reservoir, an aquarium heater will work well.

If the temperature is too hot, try adding clean ice packs to the reservoir. Wrapping the reservoir in foil to deflect heat is another option that is both easy and inexpensive. If these methods don't work, you can purchase a water chiller. This is a coiled element that cools water. It can be installed in the reservoir to keep the temperature down.

HUMIDITY

Humidity and temperature are not the same thing. They serve separate purposes and both need to be monitored closely. Your plant's needs will change over time. Keep this in mind when checking temperature and humidity levels. Different types of plants also have different needs.

During the initial growth stage of a seedling the humidity needs to be above 80%. This is only for when the seeds are germinating. After this, the humidity should be lowered to promote plant growth.

For most plants, ideal humidity is between 50 and 65%. It must be at least 45%. Humidity can be hard to control. However, as you read in the pests and diseases section, it is extremely important. Too much humidity can be devastating for your plants. Too little can cause your plant to dry out. One of the best pieces of advice regarding humidity is to get a hygrometer for your grow space!

Seasonal temperatures where you live can affect the humidity of your grow space, even if it is indoors. The ventilation in your space will also have a huge impact on the humidity. Check humidity on a regular basis to account for natural fluctuations.

If you need to add humidity, get a vaporizer or humidifier. Another option, although not a great one, is to use a spray bottle and spray water around the room. It isn't a very good option because it will get all your equipment wet as well. If you need to decrease the humidity, the best option is to increase ventilation. Increased air flow will sweep away excess moisture in the air. A simple fan (or two or three) will work wonders. Dehumidifiers or air conditioners also do an excellent job of reducing humidity.

Humidity is also affected by the number of plants being grown and how densely they are arranged. Many plants close to one another will create a windbreak that doesn't allow fresh air to flow through. If the plants are spaced too closely together, the water vapor they exude will have nowhere to go.

If you'd like to get a little fancier, you can hook up a hygrometer to a fan and have it run automatically when it senses increased humidity.

INSPECT THE EQUIPMENT

Pumps, timers, aerators, tubing, and connectors can all fail. Plus, it can take hours or days before your plants begin to show the effects caused by malfunctioning equipment. Checking your equipment regularly will prevent situations before they reach challenging proportions.

LOOK AT YOUR PLANTS!

Really look at them. Look under the leaves, examine the roots, take notice of any abnormalities on a day-to-day basis. Monitor growth patterns. If you are keeping a close eye on them, you will notice when things look off or when something has gone wrong.

Check the water levels regularly and test the nutrient levels and pH regularly. Every 3-4 days at a minimum. Every day is better.

TAKE NOTES!

Check on your plants. Take note of how much nutrient solution they are using, how big they are growing, which nutrients you are using, and how much water they are getting if they're on a timer. You won't regret this, I promise. After you have completed one grow cycle, it helps 100-fold with your next cycle to have detailed notes of what worked and what didn't, as well as any problems that were encountered and how they were overcome.

CHANGE ONE THING AT A TIME

When you are making adjustments to your system, change only one thing at a time. If you change multiple things, it becomes hard to know exactly what fixed the problem. And, if your changes cause another problem, it will be difficult to ascertain exactly why. Make changes in increments. Record the results each time.

CHAPTER 4: POTENTIAL PROBLEMS AND HOW TO OVERCOME THEM

While we'd all like to hope that our plants and systems won't encounter any of these issues, it's good to know the signs so you can easily identify them if they do occur. A lot of the pests and diseases you may encounter in hydroponic gardening are the same as those you would encounter with soil gardening. Since the hydroponic system is relatively closed and protected, your chances of encountering these problems are less than if you were gardening in soil. However, there are other problems which are unique to a hydroponic system. As with any type of gardening, diligence will go a long way towards keeping your system strong and your plants healthy.

PESTS

The potential for pests in a hydroponic system is lower than in a soil-based system. This doesn't mean that it is impossible to get them though. The main issue with pests is that because the system is so interconnected, if the problem goes unnoticed or unattended to, the end result can be devastating. Make sure you understand the telltale signs for each type of pest so that if you do see something unusual, you can act on it immediately.

Thrips

Thrips are tough to see because they are so small. However, the damage they cause is hard to miss. If your plants are infested with thrips, tiny metallic black spots will appear on the tips of the leaves. Following this, the leaves will turn yellow, then they will turn brown and dry out. Thrips are parasitic insects that leech the life from your plants, preventing them from nourishing leaf growth.

Aphids

Commonly referred to as plant lice, aphids suck the juice of leaves, turning them yellow. Aphids can be green, black, or gray. They are usually found gathered around plant stems.

Spider Mites

Unfortunately, these common pests are almost impossible to notice until you see the damage to your plants as they are so tiny. To determine if you have a spider mite infestation, check for spider-like webbing around the leaves and stem. Also, gently wipe the underside of the leaves with a tissue and check for spider mite blood.

Fungus Gnats

The larvae of this pest are what cause the damage. Adult gnats are not harmful to your plant at all. However, the larvae feed on roots and can stunt growth, cause infections, and ultimately kill the plant.

White Flies

These are relatively easy to spot because they look like very small white moths. The problem is that they fly away when disturbed and are hard to catch. They will cause white spots and yellowing of your plants.

How to Combat Pests

- Place sticky traps around the room and at the base of your plants. Yellow sticky traps are good for catching fungus gnats and white flies. Blue sticky traps attract thrips.

- Pesticides and sprays are good options as long as they are not poisonous or potentially harmful to you or your plants. Look for organic options.

- Beneficial predators such as nematodes, can be placed into your growing medium so they can hunt and kill any pests.

- Inspect your plants regularly! Don't neglect the base of the stem or underneath the leaves.

DISEASES

In general, the probability of diseases in hydroponics is less because there is no soil to encourage or start them. Fungus and bacteria thrive in soil. The most common cause of disease in a hydroponic system is environmental conditions. While this requires constant monitoring, it also means that it can be controlled. Diseases are likely to spread in crowded conditions, so make sure the plants have enough space to grow individually and that you can take out infected plants if necessary.

You can also protect your plants from disease by introducing root stimulators to your system during the early growth stages. These are the equivalent of probiotics for your plants. Trichoderma, enzymes, and thiamine can also be helpful in combating harmful pathogens and keeping your plants' immune systems strong.

Your plants will be better able to resist pathogens if they are supplied with enough nutrients (not too little and not too much) and the pH level of the system is kept within healthy parameters. Imbalances will weaken the plants' immune system, making them susceptible to opportunistic pathogens.

As with pest issues, it is best to avoid the use of any harsh chemicals. They can get into your nutrient solution, accumulate in the leaves and stems of your plants, and cause poisoning. If you must use strong chemicals, cover your water supply and spray as sparingly as possible.

ROOT ROT

This disease causes your plants to wilt and turn yellow. The roots will often turn mushy as well. It is caused by too much water and/or pathogens in your growing medium. To avoid root rot, keep the moisture levels balanced and follow the advice above regarding diseases.

GRAY MOLD

This starts out as small spots on the plant's leaves. Soon, the leaves turn gray and fuzzy and continue to deteriorate until the plant is mushy and brown. It is often called ash mold or ghost spot. It is caused by a fungus and is more common in humid areas.

POWDERY MILDEW

If it looks like someone sprinkled baby powder all over your plants, then you most likely have powdery mildew. This disease is a fungal infection. It will stunt plant growth, yellow the leaves, and eventually cause the leaves to drop. If left untreated, it can kill your plant. Too much humidity will encourage powdery mildew.

DOWNY MILDEW

Similar to powdery mildew, except it doesn't look like powder, downy mildew leaves white markings on your plant and causes yellowing of leaves. It occurs in overly wet weather, or when leaves are wet for too long. Downy mildew is usually found on the underside of leaves.

IRON DEFICIENCY

Iron deficiency causes the veins of the leaves to remain green while the remainder of the leaf turns bright yellow. The solution is fairly simple though. Introduce chelated iron to your nutrient solution and your plants will begin to look healthier in no time. You'll be able to find chelated iron at your local hydroponics store.

CALCIUM DEFICIENCY

If your plants are experiencing calcium deficiency, the young leaves on the plant will curl downwards. This is caused by a lack of water movement within the plant. Calcium is not in the nutrient mix; it comes from supplements or from the water itself. Humidity levels have a high impact on the amount of calcium a plant can absorb. High humidity reduces the amount of calcium a plant can take in.

RUST

Small red bumps will appear on the undersides of the leaves. The leaves will then turn yellow, then brown, and then die. This disease is caused by high humidity and is extremely contagious. Unfortunately, only harsh chemicals will treat this.

HOW TO COMBAT DISEASES

1. The best combat for any disease is prevention. Monitor closely and act quickly. Excessive humidity is the most common cause of the disease. Monitor the humidity of your grow space by buying a hygrometer. These are inexpensive and entirely worth it.

2. Keep air circulating with an air conditioner or fan so it doesn't become stale and encourage disease growth.

3. Do not over water your plants!

4. Remove any infected leaves and discard them outside or away from your grow space.

SYSTEM PROBLEMS

Hydroponic systems, whether homemade or store bought, suffer from a few common problems apart from pests and diseases. These challenges include algae bloom, nutrient deficiency, and system clogging.

ALGAE BLOOM

Algae are small aquatic plant organisms. They appear on the surface of the nutrient-enriched water and can look like a stain or a slimy film. Not all algae are green; they can vary widely in color. Algae can be green, black, red, or brown. It can smell like mold or dirt, especially as it decomposes. The problem with algae is that it consumes nutrients and oxygen in the reservoir and blocks irrigation lines, hoses, and pumps. Algae also attracts fungus gnats which like to eat the roots of your plants.

As algae are plants, they thrive under the same conditions that nurture all plants: light, nutrients, warmth, and moisture. Nutrients, warmth, and moisture can't be adjusted much in the reservoir; these are necessary and need to be maintained within parameters for optimal plant growth. Light, on the other-hand, can be controlled. Light shining into or onto the reservoir can be reduced or blocked out almost entirely.

The simplest solution is to negate the issue from the beginning. Use a reservoir that is dark colored or spray paint a clear one with a dark color. Another option is to create a light shield that fits around the reservoir. This can be made simply with cardboard, cut to fit around the sides. A removable protective sleeve is preferred so you can still see into the reservoir if needed.

Algae can also bloom on top of your growing medium, especially if you are using a top-watering method such as the Drip System. Here, you can't block the light from hitting the water solution since it is at the base of your plants.

The best way to deal with any algae growth is to clean everything. If you have algae in the reservoir, the next time you are changing out the nutrient solution, dump everything out and scrub all surfaces with a sterilizing solution. If algae appears on the growing medium, wash it thoroughly with clean water. This may be difficult if the plant is entrenched in the medium. You may have to wait until after the plants are harvested to give everything a thorough scrubbing.

Be careful of using any commercial sterilizing solutions or agents in the reservoir while the plants are growing. Since algae is a plant, anything that kills it could potentially kill your plants.

NUTRIENT DEFICIENCY

Nutrients and the lack thereof can have a massive impact on your hydroponic system. Plants depend upon nutrients for healthy growth. Nutrient deficiency often occurs if the plants use the solution more quickly than it is replaced. If you see signs of nutrient deficiency, reevaluate how often you are changing the nutrient solution or adding nutrients. You may need to replenish them more often. If adjusting the frequency of nutrient solution doesn't fix the problem, there are some other options. To reverse nutrient deficiency, supplement the enriched water with the missing nutrient. If that doesn't work, you may need to change the type or brand of nutrient solution you are using.

It can be difficult to identify a nutrient deficiency and the specific nutrient which needs to be supplemented. A deficiency of one element can lead to a deficiency in another, leading to a cascade effect and confusing symptoms. Often, any deficiency is an indication of a larger problem with your system. Try to look for the source of the problem as well as treating the symptom. Below is a list of the vital nutrients and the signs of specific deficiencies:

Nitrogen: stunted plant growth, lower leaves are yellow, entire plant is light green

Phosphorous: plant is blue-green in color, stunted growth, dries to greenish brown and then black (don't forget, some plants naturally have blue or green leaves!)

Potassium: dead spots on leaf edges, leaves are papery in appearance, stunted growth

Magnesium: lower leaves are wilted and yellow around the edges

Calcium: new plant growth, leaves and stems all die

Zinc: the spaces between the veins of the leaves are yellowish and have a papery appearance

Iron: veins remain strong green while the remainder of the leaf is yellow

Copper: edges of leaves curl up and look blue or dark green

Sulfur: stunted, spindly growth, older leaves remain green while new ones turn yellowy green

Manganese: stunted growth, bottom leaves are checkered yellow and green

Molybdenum: stunted, malformed, yellow leaves

Boron: scorched tips on new leaves

Nitrogen Deficiency Symptoms

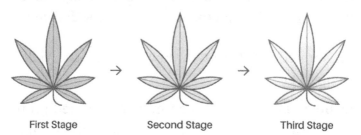

First Stage → Second Stage → Third Stage

Phosphorus Deficiency Symptoms

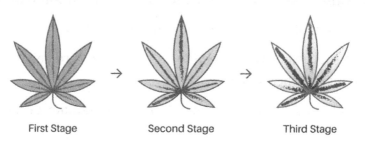

First Stage → Second Stage → Third Stage

Potassium Deficiency Symptoms

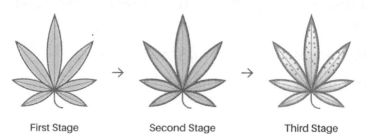

First Stage → Second Stage → Third Stage

Magnesium Deficiency Symptoms

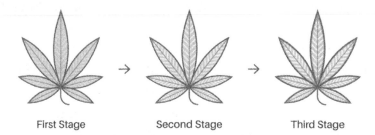

First Stage   Second Stage   Third Stage

Zinc Deficiency Symptoms

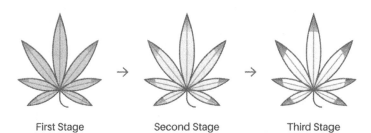

First Stage   Second Stage   Third Stage

Sulfur Deficiency Symptoms

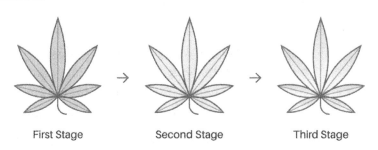

First Stage   Second Stage   Third Stage

CLOGGED SYSTEM

As discussed previously, algae is a common cause of clogged lines and pumps. If this is the case, follow the instructions above to rid the system of algae.

Lines and pumps can also be clogged if growing medium or plant matter drifts into the lines or blocks drain holes or drip emitters. To avoid this from the start, you can place filter material over any plug or hole in the reservoir or grow tray. If this is a potential issue with your system, the best solution is diligence. Monitor the pumps, drains, and drip lines. Check them daily to make sure they are working properly.

GETTING STARTED

Hydroponic systems are varied in design and complexity, in size and style, yet each one can be built by a home gardener without too much difficulty. There is a lot to bear in mind regarding nutrients, water and pH which you may not have had to pay attention to for soil-based gardening. However, once you've worked with these factors for a little while, it becomes easier. There's always a learning curve when exploring new techniques.

Hydroponic systems are a lot of fun to build and play around with. Once you've gotten comfortable with how they work, you'll be hooked. When you see how productive they are and how little space they take up compared to soil-based systems, you'll be more than pleased. The results will speak for themselves. Start off with one of the simpler systems if you're feeling hesitant and move your way up to the more complicated ones. Feel free to experiment to find out which ones work best for your location and plants. And most of all, have fun!

Appendix I – Glossary

Absorption

The intake of water and other materials through root or leaf cells.

Acid soil

Soil with a pH below 7 on a pH scale of 0 to 14. The lower the pH, the more acidic the soil. See pH.

Aeration

Mechanically loosening or puncturing soil to increase permeability to water and air.

Aeroponics

A variation of hydroponics that involves the misting of plant roots with nutrient solution.

Alkaline

Refers to medium or nutrient solution with a high pH; any pH over 7 is considered alkaline.

Alkaline soil

Soil with a pH above 7 on a pH scale of 0 to 14. The higher the reading, the more alkaline the soil. See pH.

Blight

Rapid, extensive discoloration, wilting, and death of plant tissue.

Bloom booster

Fertilizer high in phosphorus (P) that increases flower yield.

Botrytis

A fungal disease promoted by cool, moist weather. Also known as gray mold or fruit rot.

Calcium carbonate (CaCO3)

A compound found in limestone, ashes, bones, and shells; the primary component of lime.

Capillary force

The action by which water molecules bind to the surfaces of soil particles and to each other, thus holding water in fine pores against the force of gravity.

Capillary water

Water held in the tiny spaces between soil particles or between plant cells.

Chelate

A complex organic substance that holds micronutrients, usually iron, in a form that plants can absorb.

Chlorophyll

The green pigment in plants. Responsible for absorbing light energy to power photosynthesis.

Chlorosis

An abnormal yellowing of a leaf.

Clay pebble

A growing medium composed of clay that expands on contact with water, forming small round balls.

Closed system

A hydroponic system, such as nutrient film technique (NFT) systems, that recirculates the nutrient solution.

Coco coir

A growing medium composed of ground coconut husks.

Damping-off

A disease caused by many different organisms. In the most conspicuous cases, a seedling's stem collapses at or near the soil surface, and the seedling topples. Another type rots seedlings before they emerge from the soil or causes seeds to decay before germinating.

Defoliation

The unnatural loss of a plant's leaves, generally to the detriment of its health. Can be caused by high winds, excessive heat, drought, frost, chemicals, insects, or disease.

Diatomite

A fine-grained sedimentary rock formed from consolidated diatomaceous earth.

Drip irrigation

A type of irrigation system in which each plant is fed individually with a small drip tube. The flow is regulated by an emitter common to many hydroponic systems.

Deep water culture (DWC)

A hydroponic method in which plant roots are suspended in 8" or more of nutrient-rich, oxygenated water.

Ebb-and-flow

A hydroponic system in which the plants are sub-irrigated periodically and the nutrient solution drains back to a central cistern for subsequent cycles.

Feeder roots

Fine roots and root branches with a large absorbing area (root hairs). Responsible for taking up the majority of a plant's water and nutrients from the soil.

Fertilizer

A natural or synthetic product added to the soil or sprayed on plants to supply nutrients.

Fungicide

Any material capable of killing fungi. Sulfur and copper sulfate are two common mineral fungicides.

Fungus

An organism that lacks chlorophyll, reproduces via spores, and usually has filamentous growth. Examples are molds, yeasts, and mushrooms.

Fusarium

Any of several fungal diseases that afflict plants; commonly called dry rot or wilt.

Germination

The initial sprouting stage of a seed.

Growing medium

Materials that are used in some hydroponic growing methods to support the plant's roots and, sometimes, to hold nutrients.

Herbicide

A chemical used to kill undesirable plants.

Hydroponics

A method of growing plants without soil. Plants are often suspended in water or inert growing media, and nutrients are supplied in dilute solutions.

Hygrometer

An instrument for measuring relative humidity in the atmosphere.

Hymenoptera

An insect family made up of species having four membranous wings. Includes bees, wasps, sawflies, and ants.

Insecticide

Any material that kills insects. Includes numerous botanical products, both organic and synthetic.

Lime

A rock powder consisting primarily of calcium carbonate. Used to raise soil pH (decrease acidity).

Loam

A soil composed of roughly equal measures of sand, silt, and clay particles.

Macronutrient

The major minerals used by plants in large amounts. These include nitrogen (N), phosphorus (P), potassium (K), sulfur (S), calcium (Ca), and magnesium (Mg).

Micronutrient

A nutrient used by plants in small amounts, less than 1 part per million. Micronutrients include boron, chlorine, copper, iron, manganese, molybdenum, and zinc. Also called trace elements.

Mineral deficiency

When a plant does not receive a sufficient amount of a mineral, it becomes deficient in that mineral. This interferes with the health and growth of the plant.

Mycelia

Masses of fungal threads (hyphae) that make up the vegetative body of the fungus.

Mycorrhizae

Beneficial fungi that grow alongside and through plant roots, increasing their ability to take up nutrients from the soil.

Nematode

A microscopic roundworm, usually living in the soil. Some feed on plant roots and spread disease. Others benefit plants by acting as parasites for insect pests.

Nutrient film technique (NFT)

A water culture system based upon constant flow of the nutrient solution past the plant roots. NFT uses a thin film of water flowing through the roots to provide adequate moisture and aeration.

Nitrate (NO3-)

A plant-available form of nitrogen contained in many fertilizers and generated in the soil by the breakdown of organic matter. Excess nitrates in soil can leach into groundwater.

Nitrogen (N)

A primary plant nutrient, especially important for foliage and stem growth.

N-P-K

The acronym for the three primary nutrients contained in manure, compost, and fertilizers. The N stands for nitrogen, the P stands for phosphorus, and the K stands for potassium. On a fertilizer label, the N-P-K numbers refer to the percentage of the primary nutrients (by weight) in the fertilizer. For example, a 5-10-5 fertilizer contains 5% nitrogen, 10% phosphorous, and 5% potassium.

Nutrient

Any substance, especially in the soil, that is essential for and promotes plant growth.

Nutrient solution

The water solution containing all of the essential plant elements in their correct ratios; the basic nutrient supply for plant roots.

Open (non-recirculating) system

A hydroponic system in which the nutrient solution passes only once through the plant roots; the leachate is not collected and returned to a cistern for repeated cycles.

Organic fertilizer

A natural fertilizer material that has undergone little or no processing. Can include plant, animal, or mineral materials.

Organic matter

Any material originating from a living organism (peat moss, plant residue, compost, ground bark, manure, etc.).

Oxygenation

The supplying of oxygen to a solution. Healthy plant growth requires the nutrient solution to be sufficiently oxygenated.

Parasite

Any animal or plant that lives in, or on, another animal or plant and draws nutrients from its host. Parasites are harmful to the host.

Pathogen

Any organism that causes disease. Generally used to describe bacteria, viruses, fungi, nematodes, and parasitic plants.

Peat

A soil-less medium composed of partially decomposed aquatic, marsh, bog, or swamp vegetation.

Peat Mix

A soil-less medium consisting of a mixture of peat, sand, vermiculite, and/or perlite.

Perlite

A soil-less medium made from fired volcanic pumice.

pH

A scale measuring the acidity or alkalinity of a sample. What the pH scale actually measures is the concentration of hydrogen ion (H+) present in a given substance. pH values run from 0 (the most acidic value possible) to 14 (the most alkaline value possible). pH values from 0 to 7 indicate acidity, a pH of 7 is considered to be neutral, while pH values from 7 to 14 indicate alkalinity. The scale is logarithmic, thus a difference of 1 pH unit is equal to a 10-fold change in acidity or alkalinity (depending on the direction), a difference of 2 pH units indicates a 100-fold change, and a difference of 3 pH units indicates a 1,000-fold change.

Phosphorous (P)

A primary plant nutrient, especially important for flower production. In fertilizer, usually provided in the form of phosphate (P_2O_5).

Potassium (K)

A primary plant nutrient, especially important for water uptake and sugar synthesis.

Quick-release fertilizer

A fertilizer that contains nutrients in plant-available forms such as ammonium and nitrate.

Relative humidity

The ratio of water vapor in the air to the amount of water vapor the air could hold at the current temperature and pressure.

Reservoir

The container in a hydroponic system which holds nutrient solution in reserve for use.

Rockwool

A substrate used to grow plants hydroponically; an extruded wool-like product. Formed through a process of melting rock, extruding it into threads, and pressing them into loosely woven sheets at high temperatures.

Root

Generally, the underground portion of a plant. It anchors the plant and absorbs water and nutrients.

Seedling

A young plant, shortly after germination.

Selective pesticide

A pesticide that kills or controls only certain kinds of plants or animals.

Slow-release fertilizer

A fertilizer material that must be converted into a plant-available form by soil micro-organisms.

Soil

A natural, biologically active mixture of weathered rock fragments and organic material at the earth's surface.

Soil-less mix

A sterile potting medium consisting of ingredients such as sphagnum peat moss and vermiculite.

Verticillium

Any of several fungal diseases that afflict plants; commonly called wilt.

Water culture

A hydroponic method of plant production by means of suspending the plant roots in a solution of nutrient-rich, oxygenated water.

Wilt

(1) Lack of freshness and the drooping of leaves from a lack of water. (2) A vascular disease that interrupts a plant's normal uptake and distribution of water.

APPENDIX II – IDEAL pH LEVEL FOR YOUR HYDROPONIC PLANTS

Fruit Crop	pH	Vegetable Crop	pH
Apple	5.0-6.5	Asparagus	6.0-7.0
Banana	5.5-6.5	Basil	5.5-6.5
Blackberry	5.5-6.5	Beans	6
Blueberry	4.0-5.0	Broccoli	6.0-6.5
Cantaloupe	6	Cabbage	6.5-7.0
Cherry	6.0-7.5	Carrots	6.3
Grape	6.0-7.5	Cauliflower	6.0-7.0
Mango	5.5-6.5	Celery	6.5
Melon	5.5-6.0	Chives	5.5-7.0
Peach	6.0-7.5	Cucumber	5.5-6.0
Pineapple	5.5-6.0	Eggplant	5.5-6.5
Plum	6.0-7.5	Fodder	6
Raspberries	5.5-6.5	Garlic	6
Strawberries	5.5-6.5	Kale	6.0-7.5
Watermelon	5-5-6.0	Lettuce	5.5-6.5

Rawpixel.com/Shutterstock

TABLE OF CONTENTS

OVERVIEW: TYPES OF GREENHOUSES

Type of Greenhouse	Cold Frame	Hoop House	Low Tunnel	Attached	Dome	A-Frame
Cost	$	$	$	$$$	$$	$$$
Growing Seasons	1	2	2	4	4	3
Heating Cost	Low	High	High	Low	Low	Moderate-High
Longevity	<3 years	3-5 years	<3 years	10-15 years	10-15 years	5-10 years
Foundation	None	None	None	Yes	Possibly	Possibly
Strength of Framework	Low-Moderate	Low	Low	Good	Good	Moderate
Wind Resistance	Low-Moderate	Low	Low	High	High	Moderate-High
Available Light	Good	Good	Good	Moderate	Excellent	Good

Type of Greenhouse	Post and Rafter	Half-Brick	Pit	Gothic	Portable
Cost	$$$	$$$	$	$$	$
Growing Seasons	4	4	3	3-4	2
Heating Cost	Low	Moderate	Low	Moderate-High	Low
Longevity	>15 years	10-15 years	Determined by Owner	5-10 years	<3 years
Foundation	Yes	Yes	Underground	Possibly	Non
Strength of Framework	Good	Good	Determined by Owner	Good	Poor
Wind Resistance	High	Moderate-High	High	Moderate-High	Poor
Available Light	Good	Moderate	Poor	Good	Moderate

182

INTRODUCTION

Greenhouse gardening is a rewarding way to grow your own vegetables, herbs and fruits and one that I hope you will enjoy as much as I do. The best thing about a greenhouse is that you don't need a patch of land in order to grow amazing crops. It can be as small and simple as you like or as complex as you can imagine.

By definition, a greenhouse is a structure within which you grow plants. It consists of a frame covered by a transparent glazing, such as glass or plastic sheeting. Greenhouses use the sun to create a warm, beneficial, growing environment. They also protect plants from the elements, pests, diseases, and allow for longer growing seasons. There are many types of greenhouse structures. They are categorized by the amount of additional heat they provide and then further categorized by the actual type of structure.

Greenhouse-like structures go back to the days of the Romans. During cold weather, Roman gardeners stored vegetable plants under frames covered in an oiled cloth. They also planted vegetables in carts that could be moved outside during the day and inside at night to protect them. There are texts from 15th century Korea describing greenhouses designed to manage temperature and humidity for optimal plant growth. Greenhouses became known in parts of Europe in the 17th century. These early greenhouses took a lot of effort to manage. Balancing the heat was a huge problem and closing them up at night or winterizing them was complicated. Charles Lucien Bonaparte, a French botanist in the early 1800s, is said to have created the first modern greenhouse. These greenhouses were called orangeries since they were mainly used to protect orange trees from harsh, freezing temperatures. Greenhouse design continued to develop during the 17th century in Europe, but the Victorian Era is when they really began to take off. They were often elaborate structures built for the wealthy to showcase their gardens.

Since then, greenhouses have become a common sight in home gardens. Their size, design, shape, and function have changed and adapted through the years, and still today, there are new innovations for better, more efficient and effective greenhouses. Most recently, the availability of polyethylene film, or heavy plastic sheeting, has radically changed how greenhouses are built. Previously, they were almost exclusively built using glass, which works well but has limitations, such as its fragility. The introduction of PVC pipe and lightweight aluminum frames has also significantly changed greenhouse building.

The main purpose of most greenhouses, especially if they are cold-frames, is to get an early start on the growing season. This means that it gets used as an interim stage before seedlings are actually placed in the garden. Many vegetables can be started in your house or other inside location under grow lights and when they're big enough, they can be moved out to the greenhouse. Once the outside temperature is warm enough, they can then be planted in the garden. Peppers and tomatoes can be started as early as January or February inside when they have a greenhouse to relocate to after they have begun growing. This means they will be ripe a month or so before any similar plants grown without a greenhouse. Greenhouses are also used to grow plants all year round in a controlled environment. They are closed off from the elements which makes them perfect incubators for many plants. Another popular reason for using a greenhouse is to grow fruits and vegetables in the cold winter months. This usually requires a heated greenhouse, yet there is some flexibility, and a lot can depend on the temperature where it is located.

CHAPTER 1: TYPES OF GREENHOUSES

A professional greenhouse builder or gardener might take issue with what is being called a greenhouse. The term greenhouse, to most people, means a structure that holds plants and protects them from the elements while encouraging good growing conditions. A seasoned greenhouse user or a professional gardener, however, makes a very important distinction as to what constitutes a greenhouse and what doesn't.

Is it a greenhouse or a cold frame?

OVERVIEW OF DIFFERENT TYPES OF GREENHOUSES

Simply put, a greenhouse is a structure that has the means to provide internal heat. Any structure that does not have that ability is a cold frame. Cold frames provide protection, yet do not have any heating systems, relying almost exclusively on that which comes naturally from the sun.

An easy way to think of it is that a real greenhouse has a heating system installed that can run year-round if needed. It heats the entire greenhouse and keeps a consistent temperature. A cold frame doesn't have such a system installed. This doesn't mean a cold frame is without heating options. Frost covers, heat mats, cloches, portable heaters, and bubble wrap are all tools available for the cold frame greenhouse. These devices provide a small amount of heat, usually in a very concentrated manner and do not heat the entire greenhouse.

In the eyes of professional gardeners, a greenhouse allows the gardener to control the temperature and environment in ways that aren't possible with a cold frame. In this definition of greenhouses, there are three types: hothouse, warm house, and cool house. The difference between these three types lies in where it is located and the temperature maintained inside it. A hothouse has a minimum temperature of 60°F. A warm house has a minimum temperature of 55°F, and a cool house has a minimum temperature of 45°F. The key to these designations, and what sets them apart from cold frames is that the temperature is controlled and maintained throughout the entire greenhouse.

A greenhouse that grows plants year-round in a cold climate will need to have supplemental heating. The type of greenhouse heating that you need will depend on your climate and what you are growing. In places with a mild climate, you may only need to provide a little heating, or even none at all. Growing tomatoes, cucumbers, flowers and tropical plants will require a hothouse in places where the temperature gets quite low. A location with warm seasonal weather year-round can grow these same vegetables and flowers in a cold frame, using only the sun as heat. A greenhouse structure can be a cold-frame in the summer when the sun is sufficient for heating. Then, in winter, it can be turned into a hothouse or warm house to grow plants regardless of the temperature outside.

Many cold frame structures cannot be turned into real greenhouses, even if heat is added. Lack of proper ventilation for a heated space is a huge consideration. If the structure is small, any added heat can cook the delicate plants. Cold frame structures with single-pane glass, plastic sheeting, or polycarbonate windows do not provide any insulation. Any heat that is added will quickly dissipate, negating its addition in the first place.

This gets confusing though, because the term cold frame is also used to describe a certain type of structure. According to professional gardeners, a hoop house is a type of cold frame, as is a low tunnel and often a dome as well. An attached greenhouse, A-frame, or traditional style can be a cold frame or have heating to make it a greenhouse.

To the average gardener, this is confusing, and so in this guide, we will try to keep it simple. We will continue defining a greenhouse as any structure that holds plants. Just be aware that not everyone identifies it like this.

If you are looking into purchasing a greenhouse, a great way to decipher whether you are looking at a greenhouse or cold frame is to ask where a ventilation fan can be installed. A cold frame will not have a place for a ventilation fan to be permanently installed. Another great tell is the price. Greenhouses that provide internal heat are a lot more expensive, generally never less than $1,000.

COLD FRAME

A cold frame provides protection for the plants from the physical elements, like snow, rain, storms and frost. However, it doesn't have any additional heating installed, so if the outside temperatures are low or freezing, then the plants will freeze as well. Cold frame structures can still take advantage of frost covers, heating pads and other measures to help their seedlings along.

Cold frame structures are used a lot in the springtime to house plants before they are planted in a garden. They act as an in-between to harden the plants off. Seedlings that have been started inside a house cannot go straight from that environment out to the garden. They need a week or so to gradually acclimate to the change in temperature and the elements. Once the outside temperature is above freezing, a cold frame greenhouse can be used to start seedlings. The heat from the sun during the day keeps it warm enough for the seeds to sprout and flourish.

A cold frame greenhouse can also be beneficial in the fall to extend the growing season. When the temperatures outside are starting to get really cool, the heat from the sun is still enough to keep the plants growing for a while.

Plants can be put right in the ground and covered with a cold frame structure as well. Even in the winter, the heat from the sun during the day is often enough for some plants to thrive.

Cold frame structures are usually only good for two-three weeks in the spring and then another two-three weeks in the fall. Their use is limited in many ways; however, in climates where those two-three weeks make a big difference in plant growth, they are extremely useful. For the minimal expense of building such a structure, the reward can be quite great.

Since gardeners are generally an adventurous type, there has been lots of experimentation using cold frames to grow plants throughout the winter. See the section on winter gardening for more information.

COLD FRAME

Ideal for spring-time to house plants

Bildagentur Zoonar GmbH/Shutterstock.com

COLD FRAME GREENHOUSE

This type of greenhouse is placed directly in the garden. It is small and portable, so it can be moved around to accommodate different sets of plants.

Cold frame greenhouses are greenhouse building at its simplest. A sheet of plastic anchored over the plants in the garden is the easiest cold frame structure. A cold frame structure is most often a box with a hinged lid. The lid has transparent windows, usually made with glass. Recently, polycarbonate has been a popular choice because it doesn't break as easily as glass. Shattered glass in a garden is not something anyone likes to deal with.

This is as low-tech as it gets with minimal effort expended. The cost to create a cold frame greenhouse is small and can be as simple as buying plastic sheeting. The type of structure you build is completely dependent on your budget. This is a favorite choice among DIY gardeners since it is so adaptable and easy to create.

These types of greenhouses are used in the spring and fall to extend growing seasons. In the spring, they can help seedlings to stay warm and help them grow before they would normally be planted outside. The sun heats the plastic or glass, keeping the ground and plants warm underneath the covering. There needs to be ventilation in case it gets too hot, and the common method for ventilating cold-frames is propping up the door of the structure. It is possible to cook the plants if they aren't checked often. This is the biggest downside to this type of structure as it is quite easy to overheat the plants with a cold frame structure.

It is common to see old pallets being re-used as a frame. Old window frames are also a common choice.

Cold frames are a great starter greenhouse. They range in size, and you can buy one pre-made or make one yourself.

HOOP GREENHOUSE (HIGH TUNNEL)

Hoop greenhouses are becoming very popular among gardeners. They consist of a heavy sheeting plastic draped over a long-arched frame. The frame is usually made of PVC pipe or wire. They are well-liked for their versatility. They can be a permanent structure, secured to the ground and covering the crops in your garden, they can be attached to a raised bed or built to be portable.

High tunnel greenhouses are almost the same in construction to hoop houses; however, they are usually made with a steel frame and can be much bigger and longer. Many have roll-up side walls to help with ventilation. Also, in a high tunnel greenhouse, the plants grow in raised beds instead of directly in the ground.

A hoop house is similar in function to a cold frame structure; however, its design is different, and it uses different materials. Neither of them has additional heating, and both are limited as to what they can do. The main purpose of both types of structures is to harden off new plants and provide extra time in the growing season.

Tim Masters/Shutterstock

The pros are that they are easy to build and easy to adapt for size and location. Snow and rain slide easily off the roof because of the curved shape. They are inexpensive compared to many other designs.

They are not as sturdy as an A-frame or post and beam structure. In places with high winds, a hoop house will have to be very carefully secured, and they may not be an option at all in some areas.

LOW TUNNEL GREENHOUSE (CATERPILLAR TUNNEL)

A low tunnel greenhouse is a mini hoop greenhouse. It has a rigid structure of pipe bent into an arc over the garden rows and is generally covered with row cover material or plastic. It only stands about 2'-3' high. It covers the crops in the garden just enough to protect them from the elements and pests. A caterpillar tunnel is larger, usually about 6'-8' high and 10'-20' wide. They are held in place in the garden over the vegetables with ropes and stakes.

The main difference between these types of greenhouses and a hoop house is that they are removed from the garden when not in use. They are much simpler in design and less expensive to build or buy. They are also less durable and will most likely have to be replaced on a semi-frequent basis.

LOW TUNNEL

Simple in design and inexpensive to build

Tetiana_u/Shutterstock.com

The function of low tunnels and caterpillar tunnels is similar to cold frame greenhouses in that they offer protection against the elements and not much else. The biggest difference, and it's a big one, is in its design. A cold frame structure has walls and edges and a frame that blocks light from entering. Low tunnel greenhouses have no wall or roof, so when the sun is out, the plants are receiving the light fully. When you are growing in the early spring, or even winter, this makes a huge difference to the success of your garden.

Low tunnel greenhouses are also larger than cold frames. This means you can grow a larger harvest, or you can start a lot more crops earlier. Low tunnels are also lighter in weight and can be moved around your garden space more easily.

Like hoop houses, low tunnel and caterpillar greenhouses need to be secured well, or they can be blown away. They are not always an option for places with high winds.

ATTACHED GREENHOUSE (LEAN-TO)

This type of greenhouse shares a wall with an existing structure, hence the name 'attached'. Often, they are built onto the south-facing side of a house. They are also often attached to sheds, barns, and garages. They can be large or small, taking up the whole side of your house or just a small portion of your porch or deck.

The benefits of sharing a wall with an existing structure are many. Construction costs are generally lower than stand-alone structures since there is one wall already in place. Heat, water, and electricity are usually nearby and easily accessible. This is very practical and eliminates a lot of initial stress about providing heat for your plants and how to water them. They need to be watered every day, so if getting water to them is an issue, it can be overwhelming. The 8th principle of Permaculture states, "Integrate rather than segregate." In this situation, having your plants next to your living space helps you to integrate their care into your daily life and routine. It becomes less of a burden to look after them, the less you need to travel to get to them.

LEAN-TO

Benefits from existing re-sources

uncredited/Shutterstock.com

The main downside to an attached greenhouse is that it may become hard to regulate the temperature inside. The wall that the greenhouse shares with the other structure may collect the sun's heat. Also, the sun can only come from three sides, limiting the plant's exposure to light.

An attached greenhouse is generally constructed with glass windows. Recently, however, some greenhouse kits are using twin-wall polycarbonate glazing panels because they are less expensive and do a good job.

A window-mounted greenhouse is a type of attached greenhouse that is built into the window frame of a house. These are small and compact. They can be attached so that they can be accessed from inside, outside or both.

DOME GREENHOUSE

Dome greenhouses get their name from their shape: they are shaped like a dome. The frame is made up of triangulated sections with plastic sheeting covering them. This means that there is no separate roof or walls; it is all one surface with light coming in from all directions.

These types of greenhouses have a lot of great benefits. They are lightweight, sometimes portable, and stable in wind and snow. The strength of the triangle frame makes it sturdier than many other greenhouses. There are no internal supports, and the triangles distribute the weight of the frame evenly throughout. Dome greenhouses are reported to survive earthquakes, tornadoes, and hurricanes. In wind storms, the air flows around the shape of the dome instead of pushing against it. In areas where snow accumulation is an issue, these greenhouses are great. The snow slides easily off the curved structure, unlike a rectangular structure, where the snow will build up on top of it.

The biggest draw to this design is the space. The shape of the dome allows the space to be maximized for growing; vertical gardening can be achieved in the space too. The curved dome also maximizes exposure from the sun, which makes it an ideal greenhouse. With this type of structure, it isn't necessary to seek out a south-facing position.

DOME

Uses space effect-tively

Undise/Shutterstock.com

Dome greenhouses also use energy and circulate air more efficiently. The surface area of a building dictates its heat loss, and with the dome, the round surface is significantly smaller than traditional rectangular structures.

The cost of building a dome greenhouse depends on the materials you use. They can be built quite inexpensively. If you decide to build your own, search online for a "dome calculator." These programs let you enter your desired features and will then generate a diagram for you with the correct angles and dimensions.

A-FRAME GREENHOUSE

The allure of this design is its simplicity and relative ease of assembly. An A-frame is shaped like a large tent. It doesn't use as many materials as some of the other greenhouse types. A-frame greenhouses are generally built with glass windows or walls.

A-FRAME

Simplicity and ease of assembly

Marina Lohrbach/Shutterstock.com

Type of Greenhouse	Cold Frame	Hoop House	Low Tunnel	Attached	Dome	A-Frame
Cost	$	$	$	$$$	$$	$$$
Growing Seasons	1	2	2	4	4	3
Heating Cost	Low	High	High	Low	Low	Moderate-High
Longevity	<3 years	3-5 years	<3 years	10-15 years	10-15 years	5-10 years
Foundation	None	None	None	Yes	Possibly	Possibly
Strength of Framework	Low-Moderate	Low	Low	Good	Good	Moderate
Wind Resistance	Low-Moderate	Low	Low	High	High	Moderate-High
Available Light	Good	Good	Good	Moderate	Excellent	Good

The biggest downside is that because the walls narrow, the usability of the space is limited. Also, there can be issues with air-circulation in the four corners.

TRADITIONAL GREENHOUSE (POST AND RAFTER)

This design, along with the A-Frame style, is the most popular choice for greenhouses. The post and rafter greenhouse is strong and dependable. The rafters provide great support to the roof, and the design of the walls makes it easy to utilize all the space inside efficiently. The air circulation is good in this type of structure as well.

Because it is top heavy, this type of greenhouse must be footed, which is an additional expense and construction that you won't need with an A-frame.

POST & RAFTER

Strong and dependable

Mohit Chauhan Photography/Shutterstock.com

HALF-BRICK GREENHOUSE

Years ago, greenhouses with a brick foundation were very popular because, with a brick base, not as much glass was needed to complete the greenhouse. This was good because the glass was expensive. This type of greenhouse went out of style for a while, yet recently has begun to make a bit of a comeback because there are some definite benefits to the design besides the lower cost.

Bricks absorb heat. During the day, when the sun is shining down, the brick base takes in the heat and prevents the inside of the greenhouse from getting too hot. The bricks retain the heat from the day which helps to keep the temperature of the interior stable during the night and not drop too low.

Secondly, these greenhouses look good. They complement your garden aesthetically in ways that other greenhouses don't.

HALF-BRICK

Bricks retain the heat and help to regulate temperature

Alison Hancock/Shutterstock.com

PIT GREENHOUSE

This type of greenhouse is built largely underground. The interior of the greenhouse is below ground while the roof is above ground. The roof has panels of either glass or plastic to provide heat and light, like any other greenhouse. The inside walls can be built of stone, mud brick, or other material that will absorb heat and keep the greenhouse warm.

In daylight, the earthen walls of the greenhouse store up the heat. At night, they release that heat and keep the interior space warm. Above ground greenhouses only get the benefit of natural heat storage from one side, the ground. Whereas pit greenhouses utilize the four underground walls and the ground itself for heat storage. This type of greenhouse is highly energy efficient.

Another benefit of this type of greenhouse is increased protection from the elements. The downsides are the cost of digging a trench and building a foundation. Drainage is also an important issue to be considered.

If your property has a high water table, this is obviously not a good choice, or you'll have a flooded greenhouse. A pit greenhouse should be built at a minimum of five feet above the water table.

GOTHIC GREENHOUSE

The signature design of a gothic greenhouse is its curved roof. It has a semicircular frame, like half of a teardrop, that is usually covered in plastic sheeting. The technique used in building this type of greenhouse makes structural trusses unnecessary. In addition, fewer construction materials are needed which reduces costs.

GOTHIC HOUSE

Water and snow run off the roof easily

HikoPhotography/Shutterstock.com

The benefit to this design stems from its unique shape. Water and snow run off the roof easily, and it can withstand strong winds and heavy snow. Also, it conserves heat nicely. However, the downside of this design is also related to the shape. While the center of the greenhouse is tall under the arch, which is great for tall plants, the low side walls limit the planting space.

PORTABLE GREENHOUSE

Several of the options in this list are types of portable greenhouses. Cold frames and hoop houses are often built with the intention of moving them around as needed. However, there is another type of portable greenhouse that is becoming readily available and popular around the world. These greenhouses are usually a wire frame with shelving, covered with plastic, and with some type of entrance. They look like a camping or pop-up tent with shelves inside and transparent covering. Many of them use rope and stakes to secure them to the ground. They come in a variety of sizes, some not more than 4'x6'.

PORTABLE

Inexpensive, easy to set up and portable

Gyvafoto/Shutterstock.com

These greenhouses can be found in most garden supply stores and are easily assembled and set up. The upside is their lightness and portability. They can be folded up and stored like a tent each season. When you are ready to set it up, it doesn't take long, and you can choose (and change) where you want it. The downside is that they generally are not that sturdy since they aren't attached to a base. There are options that are more heavy duty than others, so if you are looking for one, make sure to research that.

Type of Greenhouse	Post and Rafter	Half-Brick	Pit	Gothic	Portable
Cost	$$$	$$$	$	$$	$
Growing Seasons	4	4	3	3-4	2
Heating Cost	Low	Moderate	Low	Moderate-High	Low
Longevity	>15 years	10-15 years	Determined by Owner	5-10 years	<3 years
Foundation	Yes	Yes	Underground	Possibly	Non
Strength of Framework	Good	Good	Determined by Owner	Good	Poor
Wind Resistance	High	Moderate-High	High	Moderate-High	Poor
Available Light	Good	Moderate	Poor	Good	Moderate

CHAPTER 2: CONSTRUCTING A GREENHOUSE

There are several ways to build a greenhouse. You can build one yourself if you are handy or know someone who is. Hoop and cold frame greenhouses are not too difficult and can be finished in a day. If the greenhouse you want is large or requires a foundation, you can hire contractors to build it. There are also many greenhouse kits available online and in gardening stores. Some kits require little to no skill to set up while others will need some construction knowledge to install.

When thinking about building or setting up a greenhouse, investigate the building codes for your area. Portable greenhouses, hoop houses, tunnel greenhouses, and small structures likely won't require any special permits. An attached greenhouse or post and rafter probably will.

DIY

Building your own greenhouse is usually the least expensive way to get the exact greenhouse you want. There are multiple places where you can buy greenhouse plans, or you can sketch and construct one of your own design. This is not always the absolute cheapest choice since it depends on what you want to build. Building materials can get expensive. Plus, the time involved in digging and setting up a foundation and doing the actual construction can add up fast. It is usually best if you have assistance when building your own. Some elements of construction can be difficult for one person.

Of course, the biggest benefit of building your own greenhouse is getting the size and style that you want. You could even combine styles if you wanted to and create your own aesthetic. It can also be designed for a specific type of plant. If the place where you are building the greenhouse is tricky or has specific requirements, this may be your only option. Building your own greenhouse will necessitate having some construction experience or the willingness to spend a lot of time researching and learning. As with most other DIY projects, the time involved in researching, designing, setting up, and then building the greenhouse is extensive when compared to buying a kit.

If you want an attached greenhouse or post and rafter structure, it will likely be necessary to hire someone to build it. The benefit to this is that it will be professionally done.

Building hoop houses and tunnel greenhouses is quite simple and can be completed in a short amount of time with a few helping hands. The supplies are generally inexpensive too, making this a rewarding DIY project.

GREENHOUSE KITS

A quick search online may overwhelm you with all the choices for greenhouse kits. There are a plethora of options for size, style, and price. Some only require a simple snapping together of pieces to assemble them, while others will need all kinds of tools and possibly some construction experience. The one you choose may depend on your own construction skills and knowledge.

Be sure to understand exactly what is needed for the assembly before purchasing the kit. It will be frustrating to find the perfect greenhouse, only to be stalled when you get it out of the box because it is too complicated or difficult for your skill level. If possible, ask the manufacturer for a copy of the manual to read before you buy it to ensure you understand it. If the greenhouse build is going to be a weekend project, check with the company to see if they have customer service on the weekend in case you run into a problem.

Check out all the features of the greenhouse before buying. Does it have ventilation? How much floor space is there? How structurally sound is it? Will it withstand weather conditions in your climate? Does it need a foundation? Will it fit in the space you want to put it? Does the greenhouse benefit the plants you intend to grow?

Many greenhouse kit manufacturers allow you to select custom options. Of course, the more specialty choices, the more expensive the greenhouse. Do your research and find the best one for you.

Greenhouse kits range in size and price. Larger greenhouse kits run approximately 8x20 and cost thousands of dollars. Smaller greenhouse kits can be as little as 27"x18" and cost less than $50.

When you get your kit, check for any damage before beginning construction. It will be hard to get the whole kit replaced, or a specific part replaced when you are in the middle of the assembly. Read the instruction manual before starting.

USED GREENHOUSES

Sometimes, plant nurseries sell their old greenhouses, or a property owner may not want a greenhouse on their property anymore and so are looking to get rid of it. It doesn't happen too often, since well-made greenhouses can last a while. Buying a used greenhouse can save you lots of money; however, as with all used goods, it can also be a money pitfall.

Do your research! Ask the owner how it was used and for how long. Assess the greenhouse for damage. If it has plastic sheeting, it will likely need to be replaced. Also, since the greenhouse has already been constructed, it will need to be taken down and moved. This may be quite expensive and complicated depending on the type of greenhouse. Additionally, it is unlikely the owner will still have the manual, so you may have to find one online or do it by best estimation. It is best to buy a greenhouse that you can dismantle yourself before moving it. This way, you can see how it goes together. Buying a greenhouse that is already disassembled could quickly become a nightmare to put back together. Taking pictures of the greenhouse before you dismantle it will be a huge help. Having some construction knowledge will also be extremely useful.

HOW TO SAVE MONEY BY BUILDING YOUR GREENHOUSE

The easiest way to save money building a greenhouse is to thoroughly assess all the options beforehand so when you start building; you aren't coming up against any unanticipated scenarios. Making multiple trips to the hardware store is frustrating and time-consuming. Discovering you don't have the right tools, materials, or instructions can cause long, frustrating, delays. Triple check the location, the size, the building method and that you have the necessary help on the day you plan to build.

If you are building from your own design, check around to see what items you already have available that will work in your build. Do you have brick, wood, windows, or plastic left over from other projects that can be used? Ask around friends and family as well to see if they have any leftover building materials you can use.

Throughout the next chapters, I will provide inexpensive options which will save you money in building and running your greenhouse.

CHAPTER 3: PLANNING FOR A GREENHOUSE

In order to decide which greenhouse works best for you, think about the space that you have, what type of plants you intend to grow, and how much money you want to spend. There is no right or wrong greenhouse. The reason there are so many types is that they have evolved to suit many different situations and budgets. A greenhouse can be a long-term investment.

If you choose an attached or A-frame greenhouse, it will be permanent. In this case, it is especially important to consider your long-term goals. Do you plan on growing the same types of plants year after year? Would you like to increase your plantings at some point? It is always best to plan for more space than you think you will need. It is better to have unused space in your greenhouse than not to have enough.

Another benefit of a larger greenhouse is that the inside temperature is easier to manage against temperature extremes. The larger the amount of thermal mass (soil) being warmed during the day, the more residual heat will be available at night to keep the plants warm.

If you are located in a snowy climate, brace your greenhouse for snow accumulation! Snow is heavy. Very heavy. If you have a lightweight greenhouse that doesn't shed snow build-up, it can collapse. Do not underestimate the weight of snow or the damage it can do.

LOCATION

If you are choosing a stand-alone greenhouse, the location should be your priority. It should be located near your garden or even in your garden. There should be access to electricity and water because you will certainly need them both at some point.

Locate your greenhouse where you will use it to its full potential. If it is too out of the way or difficult to get to, the likelihood of it being used fully is lessened.

A place where the greenhouse gets a minimum six hours of sun is necessary. In places with a cool climate, more than six hours are better. In places with hot climates, a location that provides some shade is preferred, so the plants don't get overheated. The angle of the sun changes throughout the seasons, so keep this in mind when planning your location. If there isn't a place with that much sun each day, consider adding grow lights to make up the difference.

Orient the greenhouse from east to west, so one long side will be facing south and getting the full sun each day. Nearby trees can provide necessary shade during the summer months. Then, in the winter, when they've lost their leaves, the greenhouse will get the full sun which it will need.

Trees also provide a great windbreak. Most greenhouses are lightweight which makes them function as excellent sails during wind storms. The last thing you want is your greenhouse sailing away! A sheltered location that doesn't disrupt the greenhouse's access to the sun too much is ideal.

Ensure that there is adequate drainage around the area where you build.

FOUNDATION

Whether you are building your own greenhouse or assembling one from a kit; it may need a foundation. The exceptions to this are hoop houses, low and high tunnels, portable, and cold frame greenhouses. These types of greenhouses are meant to be used directly in a garden and moved about, so there is no need for a foundation. If you are building a permanent greenhouse, though, you will need to decide on a foundation type and style.

The foundation of the greenhouse should provide anchoring, water drainage, and weed control. It needs to be anchored, so that wind gusts don't flip it over. Water needs to have a way of exiting the greenhouse. If water isn't drained, it will pool up on the greenhouse floor and attract insects, pests and promote disease. Greenhouses are an ideal location for weeds to thrive. The foundation should include measures that will prevent weed growth, otherwise, they will try to sneak in through the foundation and up through the floor. A layer of ground covering under the base will do this well. It must be landscaping weed barrier cloth, which allows water to drain through the fabric. Black plastic or tarp should not be used.

No Foundation

A greenhouse under 200 sq. ft can get away without having a foundation at all. Placing the greenhouse directly on the ground can have some real benefits, the first of which is how much easier it is. This greenhouse can be anchored to the ground with cable (see the section on securing against the wind) to keep it stable. The place you are putting it should be level. You can keep the ground as soil and plant right into the ground if you like. Alternately, a gravel or stone floor works well.

Wood

Wood is an inexpensive and simple choice. Natural decay-resistant woods, such as cedar, redwood, and cypress are recommended.

To ensure the wood doesn't rot, chemically treated wood is often recommended; however, plants absorb chemicals, so this can be problematic. A new type of pressure treated wood came on the market 15 years ago that is said to be mostly non-toxic. The plants still leach the chemicals, yet studies say it is so low it is almost undetectable. An oil finish applied to the pressure treated wood can increase safety. It is not recommended to use any treated timber from over 15 years ago.

If you do decide to use pressure treated wood, be sure to clean up any sawdust and wood shavings after building. There are many grades of pressure treated wood; the one you want for maximum durability is the ground-contact grade or whichever your lumber supplier recommends for below grade installation. If you use a different grade, then it will likely rot out fast. Even when using the correct pressure treated wood, anticipate replacing it every 8-10 years.

Alternately, if you can, the wood can be encased in concrete or other material to prevent it from being in contact with the elements and rotting.

The copper used in pressure treating is not compatible with aluminum frames as it will corrode the aluminum. A 10-mm thick barrier, minimum, needs to be placed between any pressure treated wood and aluminum.

Concrete

A 3" thick concrete slab floor works well in greenhouses. It is convenient, easy to build, and provides a flat, clean surface in the greenhouse. A drainage pipe in the center of the floor, or several spaced around, will need to be added. Water pools easily on this surface. This drain should take water to a gravel pit or use a pipe to transport it well outside the area of the greenhouse. If using a gravel pit underneath the floor for drainage, a minimum of 4" of compacted gravel or stone should be used.

A foundation needs to have footing, which is the point where the building meets the soil. The walls of the greenhouse are less likely to sag or move when there are footers. Not all greenhouses will require a footing. If they do, check with local building codes as there will be requirements regarding this. Attached greenhouses, traditional style, and A-frames will likely need a footing.

FLOOR

The flooring material in your greenhouse is important for many reasons. This is a place where you may spend hours standing and moving around, so it needs to be comfortable and caring for it should be easy. It is not something you want to have to replace often and choosing the right one from the beginning will prevent that. If the floor is uncomfortable and difficult to navigate, the joy of being in your greenhouse will be diminished.

The flooring options also span a range of costs, from basically nothing to very expensive. There is no right or wrong choice. Find the one that suits your needs and budget best.

The greenhouse floor can be made up of many materials. Sand and fine gravel are great because they provide excellent drainage. Limestone gravel is good because it is alkaline. Brick or stone slabs are aesthetically nice and work well, or you can also go down the route of keeping it dirt and using it to plant into.

Dirt/Soil

This is a nice option because it is simple. It eliminates a lot of work and saves a lot of money. Benches for plants can be set up on the floor, or you can plant directly into the soil. If the greenhouse is intended to harbor your seedlings until they are ready to be planted in your garden, you will not want to plant them directly in the soil. They will need to be transplanted, so growing containers are necessary. A greenhouse with a dirt floor can have dual uses. It can hold seedling starts during the spring and then once the garden is planted, the greenhouse floor can be planted as well. This extends your growing space and expands the types of plants that can be grown. This option is popular because it utilizes the greenhouse all year long instead of just during the spring.

Additionally, a greenhouse with a dirt floor can be used for winter growing. In this situation, planting the seeds directly into the soil is ideal. The soil will heat up under the sun during the day and warm the plants through the evening. Many other non-dirt floor options can't do this.

The soil in the greenhouse is a rechargeable battery. In the daytime, when the sun is shining at its brightest, the soil heats up and provides warmth in the space. It also stores warmth and energy. During the cooler evening and nighttime hours, the warmth slowly dissipates, like a battery losing its charge. It will take a while for this to happen; the soil doesn't lose its warmth instantly. This gives the plants heat, even when it is very cold outside. As soon as the sun rises, the soil starts to recharge and take in the heat to tide the plants over for the following night.

The biggest downside to dirt floors is they get muddy when wet. And in a greenhouse, the floor is sure to get muddy with some frequency. It can happen after you've watered your plants. If your greenhouse is located in a low spot, water can seep through the foundation. A soggy, boggy floor is not pleasant to walk on or to work in. To prevent this as much as possible, choose your greenhouse site carefully and make sure it is at a high point on your property, if possible. Carefully water your plants to avoid making too much ending up on the floor. While this may take more time, it is worth it to prevent a muddy mess.

Stone, Pavers, Gravel

Gravel or crushed stone is an inexpensive choice that suits a greenhouse well. It is easy to install, easy to clean and drains excellently. It can provide extra humidity in your greenhouse if needed; simply spray the rocks with water. Some people don't like the feel of walking on gravel because it can move around a lot under your feet. The other downside to gravel or stone is that wheelbarrows are impossible to use on it. If your greenhouse is big enough to use a wheelbarrow or dolly in, take this into consideration. Landscape rocks also work great; however, they are more expensive.

Pavers are generally used to create paths over dirt floors. This is necessary because the dirt floor will get muddy at times. They are also used to create solid walkways on gravel floors and as supports under tables and shelves. If table legs are placed directly in the gravel, they can shift and sink over time. Pavers placed underneath them prevents this.

Placing a weed barrier cloth beneath the gravel or pavers is highly recommended. A weedmat can be bought at most garden supply stores. Cheap versions of weedmats aren't always effective and might still end up allowing weeds through, so make sure you get a well-reviewed one.

Concrete

A concrete floor provides a smooth, clean surface in your greenhouse. This flooring also retains heat during the day and naturally keeps your greenhouse warm. It is easy to move plants around and rearrange containers and growing trays. It is easy to wash and is nice to walk on. If you poured a concrete foundation, this also makes a great floor, which cuts down on building time and costs.

Wood

Wooden floors are pretty; however, you will encounter the same problem with a wood floor that you would with a wood frame. Greenhouses are humid spaces, and wood floors can harbor diseases and mold. Also, they are likely to rot, even when you are using pressure treated wood meant for outdoors.

Brick

Brick is an attractive choice for a greenhouse floor as well as being practical. Clay is porous and absorbs water which will provide additional humidity to your greenhouse. A layer of sand should be laid beneath the bricks for drainage and stability.

Vinyl Tiles

Gardening supply stores sell special vinyl tile that is made for greenhouses. It is porous, drains well, and is easy to clean. Vinyl tiles are comfortable to walk on and look nice. However, they are expensive compared to other flooring options.

Mulch

While mulch is easy to acquire, cheap, and simple to install as flooring, it is not recommended for greenhouse flooring. As it breaks down, it can introduce mold and insects into your greenhouse. Also, it is not a permanent flooring and will need to be replaced every year.

Dirt & Gravel Combination

A popular method of greenhouse flooring is to install raised beds that keep the dirt floor underneath them with gravel or stone laid out everywhere else. This type of floor is ideal in many ways. The plants get the benefit of growing as deep as they need to into the dirt floor, and they also receive the warmth of the soil, which is particularly beneficial in colder months. The remainder of the greenhouse floor is cleaner and easier to walk on with gravel or stones as walkways. The downside to this configuration is that once you have built the raised beds, the design is permanent. Plants and beds can't be moved around at all, so if you choose this option, make sure you have it designed exactly how you want it.

FRAME

The type of material that is used for the frame will depend on where you are located and what type of greenhouse you want. Even if you are purchasing a greenhouse kit, it is important to pay attention to the type of frame material used. Aluminum, plastic, wood, and PVC are the most common choices.

Aluminum

Aluminum is great because it is inexpensive, doesn't rust and assembles easily. The not-so-great thing about aluminum is that it doesn't insulate, so that the greenhouse will lose heat through the frame. Aluminum can vary in strength and quality and not all aluminum frames can hold up against strong winds or heavy snow.

Plastic

Also inexpensive, plastic is a good choice for a frame. It doesn't have the insulation problem that aluminum does since it holds heat quite well. It is durable and weather resistant. The downside is that prolonged exposure to the sun can cause the plastic to expand and contract, leading it to warp. A light-colored plastic will limit this.

Wood

Wood has been used for a long time to build greenhouses and is still a popular choice. It is readily available, generally easy to work with, provides excellent strength, and is a good insulator. The thing to be wary of with wood is that because it is porous, it can be a haven for disease and mildew. Since greenhouses are damp, wet, spaces, this can be a real issue. A wooden greenhouse will need to be kept extra clean to prevent any outbreaks. The dampness in a greenhouse will likely cause the wood to rot as well, which means you will need to replace or rebuild it at some point. A high-quality, rot-resistant wood should be used such as cedar or redwood (also see information regarding pressure treated wood within the foundation section above).

PVC

The flexibility of PVC makes it a popular choice for hoop houses and tunnel greenhouses. It is simple to work with, lightweight, and inexpensive. It is also a great insulator. The downside to PVC is its lack of strength, which means it isn't great during strong winds or storms. The majority of greenhouses sold in kits use PVC frames.

Galvanized Steel

Galvanized steel is another option that is popular in areas that have heavy snowfalls or strong winds. It is extremely strong and can hold up in many weather situations. The downsides are the weight, 3x that of aluminum, and the fact that the galvanizing will wear off over time and then it will rust. If you decide on galvanized pipe, use 1 ½" pipe instead of 1" for extra strength. The 1" can still struggle to hold up under heavy snows. This is a good investment in climates where there is snow accumulation.

GLAZING

In greenhouse terminology, the type of covering around the greenhouse frame is called glazing. This is what lets the light and heat in from the sun. Traditionally, it has always been glass. In more recent times, plastic sheeting and polycarbonate have become popular as well.

Glass

The traditional option, glass, is still a great choice. It lets in light easily, keeps the space warm and is generally easy to acquire. If properly cared for, a glass greenhouse can last decades. Single-pane glass is not a good insulator which can be a problem. A double or triple pane is better, yet of course it is more expensive, and glass is already the most expensive option.

The other problem with glass is that it breaks easily. Cleaning up shards of glass from your plants or soil is not good. It can also be difficult and time-consuming to replace because of its fragility.

Plastic (polyethylene) sheeting

Plastic sheeting is great because it's inexpensive and easily available. It is the least expensive of all the options and does a good job of letting light in and holding in heat. If it gets ripped or punctured, it can be patched or replaced without too much difficulty. The biggest drawback with plastic is that it doesn't last forever. It will deteriorate from exposure to the elements and will need to be replaced every few years.

There is a type of plastic sheeting that is treated to resist ultraviolet rays. It is available at most greenhouse supply stores and is usually guaranteed for about four years. 6-mm plastic sheeting is recommended. Using two layers of this plastic as your glazing helps prolong its life a little more.

Regular utility grade plastic sheeting that is available everywhere is not recommended unless you want to replace it every year. It is the absolute cheapest and will do the job for one year. Once it starts to disintegrate though, it can become a real mess with little bits of plastic finding their way all over your greenhouse and garden. There are also other specially treated plastic sheeting options such as thermal protection, anti-condensation, and heat protection. For a greenhouse though, the UV rating is of the highest importance.

Plastic (polyethylene) panels

The same material used for plastic sheeting is also available in panels. The panels are usually double insulated, UV protected and good for about 10 years.

Acrylic

Also commonly known as plexiglass, acrylic is tough, durable, and slightly flexible. Acrylic panels can be complicated to install though because they expand and contract, so the attachments have to be very specific. It is also very expensive, about the same price as glass. Yet, it makes up for that by being extremely durable, lasting up to 20 years.

Polycarbonate tiles and rolls

Polycarbonate is the newest glazing option to become available. It is amazing in all its properties. It lets light in better than glass or plastic, holds heat well and can be used on flat or curved surfaces.

Polycarbonate is also lightweight and very strong. Panels are treated with a UV resistance to prevent yellowing and deterioration. It is less expensive than glass yet more expensive than plastic sheeting. Generally, it is guaranteed for about ten years.

SECURING AGAINST THE WIND

This is particularly important if your greenhouse is not on a permanent foundation. Cabled anchors are commonly used to secure a greenhouse. They include a set of four anchors, one for each corner, mounting hardware to secure it to the base, and cable to attach them. The anchors aren't too expensive, and if you live in a windy or stormy climate, it will be entirely worth it.

If you have a portable greenhouse, the edges can be weighed down with bricks, stone, or heavy wood pieces.

A hoop house or tunnel greenhouse can be secured with tent pegs and rope. The frame poles should already be sunk at least 2' into the ground to prevent it from blowing over in the wind.

Hoop houses and tunnel greenhouses can also billow in the wind, like sails or giant kites. Fabric strapping zig-zagged across the roof will help keep the plastic in place and prevent it from flying away.

Constructing your greenhouse in a sheltered location will also greatly reduce the chance of wind damage. Trees can provide shelter from wind, as can buildings and other structures. Building the greenhouse at a lower elevation than the land around you will also help protect it from the wind.

CHAPTER 4: GREENHOUSE ENVIRONMENT

Keeping the environment in the greenhouse steady and controlled is important for the health and productivity of the plants. Greenhouses need to provide adequate temperature levels, sunlight, and humidity. The environment that you create in your greenhouse depends on what you are growing. Some plants need lots of heat while others thrive in cooler temperatures.

HEAT

Maintaining a steady temperature in a greenhouse can be quite difficult. During the day, the glazing materials let in heat and light with ease, causing the temperature to soar. Once night comes though, all the light is gone, and the heat dissipates quickly. It can swing from 100°F during the day to 30°F at night (depending on where you live), which plants do not like. This type of fluctuation can hurt the productivity of the plants. Part of the purpose of heating is to stabilize the temperature within the greenhouse.

Tropical plants need temperatures above 70°F and high humidity. Cool-loving plants, like carrots, lettuce, radishes, peas, and beets, do well in greenhouses with a nighttime temperature of around 50°F. Tomatoes and many flowering plants like nighttime temperatures to be around 65°F. Research what temperature the plants you are growing will need, so you do not waste time and energy on heating if it isn't necessary. At the end of the book, you'll find an overview of the most common crops for the greenhouse and their temperature requirements. If you have a large greenhouse and only some of the plants need additional heat, arrange the plants together and set up the heating to concentrate on them. This will reduce your overall costs and allow you to grow a range of plants.

During cool and cold months, the temperature inside the greenhouse will fall at night. During the day, the sun will heat it enough to keep everything alive; however, once the sun is gone, so is the heat. If it is freezing outside, it will be freezing inside the greenhouse too, and your plants will not survive.

If your greenhouse is not insulated, any form of heating will be ineffective. Polycarbonate panels can keep heat in as well as double layered plastic sheeting. Of course, double layer plastic reduces light transmission, so there is a trade-off.

Heating a greenhouse can be expensive and possibly not worth the trouble or cost, depending on where and what you are planting. A goal of many home gardeners is to be sustainable, and spending a lot of money on heating is not viable. There are ways to keep heat in using minimalist methods that aren't expensive. They vary in effectiveness, and you will need to experiment a bit to see what works best for your arrangement.

Once you've decided on a type of heater, you'll need to figure out what size to get. One size definitely does not fit all since there are so many types and sizes of greenhouse. Determining what size heater to get takes a bit of math. First, you'll calculate the surface area of your greenhouse floor. Multiply the length of your greenhouse by the width to get this number. Once you know the surface area, you can seek out heating systems that cover it. Here is a greenhouse calculator you can use for your calculation:

http://www.littlegreenhouse.com/heat-calc.shtml

There are several heating options available to help your plants make it through the cold temperatures.

Propane Heater

These are generally inexpensive and are easy to set up. There are many options available to choose from. Most have several settings, so you can control how much heat is given off. There are some propane heaters designed specifically for greenhouses, but this type is of course more expensive. They are treated against rust, which is a real threat in a humid space such as a greenhouse.

Electric fan heater (220-volt)

This, of course, requires that you have access to an electrical outlet. These heaters circulate air well and help prevent cold spots and disease development. If you go down this route, get a heater with a thermostat. This way, you can set it to only turn on when the temperature reaches a particular point. When the desired temperature is reached, the heater will automatically turn off. Having a system operate on its own reduces a lot of extra work and monitoring.

The placement of the fan heater within the greenhouse makes a big difference. Centrally located, open spots are best. One big benefit of this type of heater is that it can be moved around easily and then completely removed when it is no longer needed. This is great if space is a limited commodity in your greenhouse. Depending on the cost of electricity in your area, this can become expensive.

Gas or oil heaters

These are inexpensive options that provide decent heat. Open flame gas heaters should be avoided because they release ethylene gas which negatively affects growing plants. Ethylene gas doesn't have a smell, so it is near impossible to know there is a problem until it is too late. Plants will wilt, drop their flowers, and upper leaves will be twisted and deformed.

These types of heaters have oxygen safety sensors which will turn off the heater automatically when they sense there's not enough oxygen in the greenhouse. In a home, this is a good thing. In an air-tight greenhouse, it is not. Oxygen can be depleted easily in a well-insulated greenhouse. If the heater shuts off in the middle of the night because of this, it can cause the plants to die. A gas heater with an exhaust is best, and these require an outside vent for the exhaust to pass through.

Solar heaters

Installation of the solar panels and setting up the system will likely require a professional as it will need to be custom built. The panels have a food-grade antifreeze piped through them via a circulating pump. This system has given great results to gardeners who have it.

Wood and pellet stoves

Because fuel is expensive, wood is often a popular, cost-effective means of heating a greenhouse. They require proper set-up, circulation, and venting. If your greenhouse has plastic sheeting, a wood stove is not a good idea. Heat and plastic do not mix.

These types of stoves require tending and only provide heat for as long as you are feeding them. This is not a heat source that can be turned on and left alone. Depending on the size of the stove and your greenhouse, you may have to fill it with wood every few hours. Since most greenhouse set-ups need the heating at night, this means trips in the middle of the night.

There are mixed reports on the viability of pellet stoves. They work well, provide good heat, and are easy to maintain; however, they have been known to rust and stop working. The humidity in the greenhouse is its enemy.

Radiant heat lamps

This type of heater looks like a lamp with a red light-bulb. It needs to be plugged in, so you will need access to an electrical outlet. It is hung over the plants, and its heat is sent directly downwards. They are inexpensive and come in a variety of sizes. Radiant heat lamps are best if there are only a few plants that need warming. They will not heat an entire greenhouse and don't distribute warmth anywhere but straight down.

INEXPENSIVE OPTIONS

Floating row cover

While this isn't a heater, per se, it is a means of retaining heat in your greenhouse. Drape the row cover directly over the plants and it will keep the plants several degrees warmer than the room or the outside temperature. There are several types and weights to choose from, and the one you need will depend on the plants and the time of year. It is designed to allow light in while keeping insects and diseases out. It can be cut to size, and it is easy to move around to different areas of the garden. As the plants grow, they easily push the fabric up. Row cover is reusable and generally lasts one-two seasons. It can tear easily and deteriorate if not cared for properly.

Frost blankets

Designed to protect seedlings, these are similar to row covers, yet are thicker and provide a lot more protection. They offer protection for plants down to 24°F. They can be used to extend the growing season in conjunction with a greenhouse or in place of a greenhouse.

Cloches

A cloche is another choice that is not a heater, yet will provide extra warmth to your plants. A cloche is a bell-shaped or square shaped container that is placed over the plants. Traditionally, they were made of glass, yet nowadays, they are often constructed of plastic. Most designs will provide a method of venting because it is easy for plants to overheat underneath them. They are designed to be placed over individual plants or a selection of plants.

Rocks and Bricks

An inexpensive and easy way to add some heat to your greenhouse is to place rocks inside. During the day, they will collect the sun's heat and will release the heat at night and keep the space warm. Darker colored rocks will collect more heat. These should be placed near the plants for highest effectiveness.

Bubble Wrap

This is an insulator rather than a heater. If you are looking for a low budget option to retain heat in your greenhouse, this is a good choice. Secure a layer of bubble wrap on the inside walls of the greenhouse to reduce heat loss and block draughts. Horticulture bubble wrap insulation is made specifically for this purpose and can be found at a garden supply store. It is UV treated and toughened for use.

Having an additional layer of plastic in your greenhouse will reduce the amount of light that comes in by approximately 10%. This will negatively impact the growth of your plants. Choose a bubble wrap with larger sized bubbles as this will let in more light. This only helps a little though.

Bubble wrap can be used to provide a partition between areas of your greenhouse. With partitions, you can use a heater in sections just for certain plants. This reduces wasted energy and the wasted cost of heating an entire greenhouse when you only need a small portion heated.

It is important to remember, regardless of which heater you choose, to make sure your greenhouse is vented. Also, the heating system should have an automatic shut-off.

Heated propagator mat

These are mats that can be purchased at gardening supply stores. They are set underneath pots and trays of seedlings and send heat upwards. They are electrical and need to be plugged in.

SHADE

The amount of shade a greenhouse gets is important. This may seem odd since greenhouses are designed to bring in the maximum amount of light and heat from the sun, and those that bring in the most are considered better. However, greenhouses are about microclimates and management. Sun is great. Too much sun is not great. And it will vary at different times of the year. Remember, as seasons change, so do the hours of sunlight, and this has a direct effect on the health of your plants.

Plants can be burned in the summer months when they are receiving long hours of direct light. The leaves will be discolored and look bleached. To protect them, it is necessary to provide shading of some sort. There are a variety of options such as vinyl plastic shading, roll up screens, polypropylene shade cloth, and paint on materials.

Shading is complicated by the fact that plants need light and any shade limits that. It is about finding a good balance. It is better to err on the side of caution and provide the minimal amount of shade needed. The temperature inside your greenhouse should not exceed 81°F.

External blinds

External blinds attach to the outside of your greenhouse. They provide excellent shade since they block the sun before it hits your windows. They are easy to use and are easily manipulated. Putting them all the way down or partially down is not a problem, and you can set them how you like. The biggest downside to this type of shade is their cost. They are on the expensive side. Additionally, depending on your greenhouse setup, they may interfere with the operation of your vents. External blinds can be set up on a remote.

Internal blinds

Internal blinds are not as effective as external blinds because they block the sun after it has already passed through the windows. They do work well though and are popular as a shade. Like external blinds, they are easily adjusted and can be lowered all the way or partially. And each blind can be set to a different height which gives the gardener a large amount of control. Some internal blind systems can also be controlled via remote.

Shade cloth/netting

The material used for shade cloth can vary; however, the most important thing to pay attention to with shade cloth is its filtration rating. They are usually listed as 40%, 50%, 60%, or 70% and refer to how much sunlight they will block. Which one you need depends on your particular situation. In most cases, 40%-50% is sufficient unless the greenhouse is south-facing and gets non-stop sun all day long.

Shade cloth can be hung on the interior or exterior of the greenhouse. Hanging the cloth on the outside will be more effective since it will block the sun before it hits the glazing. For some people, the aesthetics of an external shade are undesirable. An external shade cloth will also degrade quicker than an internal one since it is more exposed to the elements.

A common shade cloth material is aluminized polyester. This reflects light instead of just blocking it, making it extremely effective. Aluminum curtains can also be used at night to keep heat in.

Another popular choice is polyethylene plastic because it is inexpensive. It is usually knitted or knotted together in some fashion to form a type of cloth or cohesive material. It is UV treated to withstand the sun.

Shade cloth is attached with hooks, clips, or grommets. Manufactured options will have the attachment kit included.

This option is less expensive than blinds, however it will degrade quicker (both internal and external) and will need to be replaced more often.

Shade paint

Applied externally to the glass, these paints work quite well. There are several brands on the market to choose from. Several layers of paint can be added, depending on the needs of the season. When you don't need it anymore, it washes off. These paints are not recommended for acrylic or polycarbonate windows as they don't wash off well. Shade paints are not expensive. The main difficulty in using them is that it is hard to apply a uniform coating.

DIY shade cloth

Home gardeners have reported success using burlap cloth, and even plain white bed sheets as shade cloth. In a pinch, either of these will work well. For a long-term solution though, it is recommended to get something specifically made for shading greenhouses.

Natural shade

Trees, buildings, and structures can provide natural cooling for your greenhouse. The shadow from these objects is shading that can be counted on every day. Sometimes, it is problematic since it can't generally be moved; however, if you work the natural shade into your greenhouse plan, you can really make it work for you.

Ventilation/cooling

When the greenhouse is receiving lots of direct sun for long hours, it is possible for the plants to become overheated. This is different from burning. Overheating will cause the plants to wilt and die. Proper ventilation is also required to prevent the spread of diseases in the humid environment. Having a source of ventilation that can be manipulated as needed is extremely important.

In a greenhouse, there are three main places that air can come in and out. The first is the main door. It can be opened or closed as needed throughout the day to provide air flow. The second is roof vents, and the third is side vents.

Most greenhouses have hand-operated vents or flaps that can be opened and closed when necessary. There are also electric and temperature sensitive vent options available. An oscillating fan will provide good air flow. Some greenhouse designs, like the hoop house, can have roll-up sides which is great for ventilation. The majority of greenhouse kits will have roof and side vents already installed.

Smaller greenhouses generally have a greater ventilation need since they have a higher glass to floor ratio. There is less space for heat to spread out, and it is being heated at a fast rate, so if you purchase or build a small greenhouse, monitor the heat carefully.

To properly understand the ventilation needs of your greenhouse, a thermostat should be installed inside. A remote access one is especially handy. The temperature inside should not exceed 81°F as temperatures higher than that can cause problems with your plants.

There is no cookie cutter method to ventilating a greenhouse. As with so many things, it depends on a lot of different factors. For example, the size and type of greenhouse, whether there is access to electricity, what you're growing, and the gardener's budget. In general though, an automatic system is greatly preferred over a manual one. Having vents that open automatically makes a big difference to the welfare of your plants and your workload.

Keep an eye on the health of your plants by checking for leaf scorching, wilting, and extreme dryness. These are signs that you need more ventilation or that your current system is not working.

Passive and Powered Ventilation Systems

There are two types of ventilation systems: passive and powered. Passive ventilation systems have no mechanical parts. The most basic vents are passive. These are great in terms of simplicity, ease of use, and if noise is an issue.

A passive (also called natural) ventilation system depends on thermal buoyancy for air movement. When air is heated, it rises naturally, and as the air rises, it flows out of the roof vents. Vents installed on the side walls suck in fresh air as the hot air leaves. This ensures there is always good air circulation around the plants.

A passive system is still at the mercy of the outside temperatures. It can keep the air flowing and keep the inside temperature lower by degrees; however, it won't maintain a consistent temperature.

A passive system is not as effective as a powered one, yet it is more cost-effective than a powered system since it doesn't require electricity. It is a great choice for any greenhouse and is ideal if your greenhouse is located somewhere without access to electricity.

Powered ventilation systems incorporate fans and often temperature-controlled thermostats, so the system can turn on and off on its own. This type of system is more accurate than a passive system, and it is easier to keep the greenhouse at a specific temperature. The increase in temperature control is a huge bonus, especially if you are growing highly temperature sensitive plants. Additionally, powered ventilation systems provide a closed system in your greenhouse which means pests and debris can't get in through open vents. They are, of course, much more expensive.

Fans used in a powered system can cause quite a bit of noise. If your greenhouse is attached to the side of your house, keep this in mind when deciding which system to use. The noise levels may be disturbing.

Doors

Propped open doors are a simple, effective way to bring fresh air into a greenhouse. Every greenhouse has a door, so this is an easy option. It won't provide adequate ventilation since the air is only coming from one direction, yet it is a start. Depending on the size and layout of your greenhouse, it may only make a dent in the air flow that the plants need. However, since it's such an easy thing to do, it shouldn't be overlooked. If your greenhouse has two doors, that is much better. Propping them both open will create a good cross-breeze.

Hand operated vents

Simply put, this type of vent is either on your wall or the roof and operates with a hand crank. These vents are easy to use, don't require any special tools, electricity, or know-how. There is no equipment that can break down which makes them ideal for a simple, no-frills, greenhouse design. Most prefabricated greenhouses come with a hand crank vent.

The biggest downside to this type of ventilation, and it can be a huge hurdle for many gardeners, is that you must be there to operate it. This can require extra planning every day to ensure that the vents are opened and closed at the necessary times. If you work outside the home and aren't there to vent the greenhouse during the hottest parts of the day, it can be fatal for your plants. Particularly during the summer months, the weather will need to be checked every morning before leaving the house, and the greenhouse vented in anticipation of mid-day temperatures. It is an extra chore and is a big problem if it is forgotten.

Electric vents

These vents are the same as hand operated vents in style and size. The difference is that the vents are not opened manually. Some are attached to a control system, so you only have to press a button for them to open. This can be helpful since it will reduce the effort needed to open the vents. In a large greenhouse, this can be a key issue, especially if the vents need to be opened and closed often. Alternately, the vents can be connected to a thermostat, so that they will open and close automatically depending on the temperature inside the greenhouse.

Temperature sensitive/automatic vents

These vents are really neat and a great way to provide circulation in your greenhouse. They work via solar power and don't require any electricity. The cylinder mechanism of these vents operates through heat build-up in the greenhouse. As heat builds, the vents slowly open. When it gets cooler, the vents slowly close. It is entirely automatic, and once it's set up, requires virtually no care. They are very easy to set up. The cylinders do wear out after a while but they are easy to replace.

This type of vent operates solely on the temperature inside the greenhouse. They will not close if it starts to rain unless the rain brings a drop in temperature.

Exhaust fan

An exhaust fan will move and refresh the stale air in the greenhouse. They are usually mounted on the roof and draw the hot air up and send it outside. Exhaust fans can be motorized or non-motorized. The motorized ones are, of course, more expensive. They provide more air flow than vents, and therefore make it easier to maintain a specific temperature inside the greenhouse.

Oscillating fans

Oscillating fans are a quick, simple tool to bring air movement into the greenhouse. They are inexpensive and are extremely handy since they are portable and so can be moved around the greenhouse as needed. Having several of these on hand to focus on specific areas or plants can make a big difference.

Roll up sides (hoop houses and tunnel greenhouses)

Hoop houses and tunnel greenhouses can be simple to ventilate since the sides of the structure can be designed to roll up as needed. Some systems require manual lifting of the sides and others have automatic controls. The entire side of the hoop house can be set to roll up or just a portion of the side. Fresh air rushes in and pushes the warm air out, creating a good flow of air around the plants. The electricity costs of this type of set up are significantly less than using fans. It can be combined with a thermostat to operate automatically, raising and lowering to maintain a prespecified temperature.

Evaporative cooling mats

These mats are available at gardening stores. They use the hot air in the greenhouse to evaporate water from the plants and other wet surfaces to bring the temperature down. They can bring the temperature down 10-20°F below the outside temperature. These mats generally work best in dry climates, yet can be effective anywhere.

The mats are mounted on the wall of the greenhouse and supplied with water to keep them wet. The pads need to be continuously wet in order to work properly. Hot outside air flows through them, creating the cooling effect, or a fan can be mounted on the opposite wall to create air flow.

Cooling mats are an easy system to use once installed. They do the job automatically, so you don't have to worry about cooling. They don't need electricity or batteries.

Wireless systems

Wireless systems provide a lot of new and exciting possibilities, taking garden automation to the next level. Ventilation of the greenhouse can be monitored from a computer or cell phone, possibly through an app. These systems usually gather data as they operate which can be reviewed for possibilities of greater efficiency. Also, if there is a problem, it will be discovered sooner.

HUMIDITY

Measuring and monitoring the humidity in your greenhouse is extremely important for the health of your plants. Relative humidity is a measure of the amount of water in the air. The problem with excess humidity is that it causes the leaves on your plants to get wet. Leaves that are wet for an extended period of time are a prime location for disease to bloom. The diseases are then easily spread when moisture, caused by the humidity, builds up on the roof and drips down onto all the plants. An outbreak can happen very quickly.

Relative humidity is measured by how much moisture the air can hold. Warmer temperatures hold more moisture. A greenhouse with a temperature of 70°F will hold up to five times more moisture than the same air at 30°F. Water drops condense on cars, grass, and plants when the air reaches its saturation point, called the dew point. A psychrometer measures the humidity in the air and is a good tool to have on hand.

In a greenhouse, moisture comes from several places. It evaporates from the soil; plants give moisture off naturally, and of course, it comes from watering the plants.

To combat moisture, the best thing to do is to make sure the air inside the greenhouse is always circulating. Ventilating it will make a huge difference (see above section on ventilation). Appropriate plant spacing and watering will help a lot too and so will having well-drained floors. Keeping the greenhouse dry will also have a big impact. This is especially important when the temperature drops, as if there are puddles, they will evaporate and cause moisture build-up in the air.

It is good practice to water the plants only as much as they need, so there is no excess water pooling in the greenhouse. Watering in the morning gives the plant surfaces time to dry before the temperature drops in the evening.

The leaf canopy of your plants is where the highest relative humidity can be found. This is caused by transpiration. Transpiration is the passage of water through a plant and its evaporation through the plant's leaves, stems, and flowers. Plants adapt the amount of water they take in through their roots based on the surrounding temperature. If plants are spaced too closely together, or there isn't adequate air circulation, the moisture gets trapped in the leaf canopy. Weeds are also a big contributor to transpiration.

On hot days, plants will take in more water to keep themselves cool. When the temperature lowers at night, the water intake slows naturally. If there are sudden increases or decreases in temperature, which, in turn affects the humidity, the plants can't react fast enough and will show signs of stress. The damage to the plants can be reduced or eliminated if the plants have enough time to adjust. Take measures to reduce humidity in stages, so they have this time.

LIGHTING

The majority of light in your greenhouse will be provided naturally by the sun. During extended periods of sunless days and during the winter, you may need to supplement the amount of light your plants are getting. Plants need a minimum of six hours of light with some varieties needing a lot more to thrive. Do not give your plants more than twelve hours of light. They need downtime, and too much light will cause them to grow oddly.

Younger plants, in general, need less light than older plants. The greatest need for light when they are older is to facilitate blooming. Group plants with similar light requirements in the same area. This will make it easier to provide each plant type with the correct amount of light. You can find details on lighting requirements for each plant at the end of this book.

The lighting that you need for your greenhouse will depend on the available hours of sunlight, what time of year it is, what plants you are growing, and how much you want to spend. Many greenhouse growers install a combination of different lights for maximum benefits.

Compact Fluorescent Bulbs (CFLs)

An inexpensive and effective choice is compact fluorescent light bulbs. They are a type of light bulb that can screw directly into an existing light socket. This makes them easy to set up because they don't need special wiring. CFLs provide full-spectrum lighting, which is the same as that emitted by the sun. These light bulbs are ideal because they are similar to sunlight, and also shine the light in all directions, which is great for greenhouses. The packaging for the light bulbs will indicate the temperature range. When your plants are young, they will do well with a lower temperature rating, and when they mature, they will benefit from a higher temperature rating. And, because they are light bulbs, all you need to do is switch them out which makes things very easy.

T-5 Fluorescent Lights

These come in four-foot lengths and are installed in the ceiling above your plants. They are cost-effective, powerful, and efficient lights. Horticulture bulbs are available and come in red or blue. And, the T-5 light fixtures can often hold multiple bulbs which means you can customize the lights for your greenhouse.

The standard fluorescent light, the T-12, can be used, however it does not have the same intensity and efficiency as T-5s.

Metal Halide

This type of light has a high-intensity discharge (HID) and is more intense than fluorescent lighting. They provide the blue light spectrum that plants need for vegetative growth. The lights come in 400, 600, and 1000 watts. They produce lots of heat and consist of a bulb, ballast, and socket base. These lights work well, however they require a lot of electricity, making them a non-economical choice for many gardeners.

High-pressure sodium (HPS) lamps

Another type of HID light, the HPS lamps provide light on the red spectrum, as opposed to blue like the metal halide ones. The red spectrum is good for flowering and fruiting plants. They come in 400, 600, and 1000 watts. The set up for these lamps requires a bulb, ballast, and socket base.

Metal Halide and HPS combination

Purchasing a convertible ballast will allow you to use both a metal halide and HPS bulb in the same socket. Not at the same time though. The metal halide can be used while the plant is young and growing, and then it can be switched out for the HPS for the flowering stage.

Light Emitting Diode (LED) Light:

LED lights are extremely energy efficient which is quickly making them a top choice among greenhouse growers. Energy costs can add up fast if there is a need to have the lights on frequently. These lights are expensive; however, their long life makes up for it. They can last 8-10 years. Another benefit is that LED lights don't get nearly as hot to touch as regular light bulbs. This means they can be placed close to the plants without as much worry about the temperature.

There are LED lights designed specifically for growing plants, and they have adjustable red, white, and blue lights. For those that need precision, these are the best choice.

IRRIGATION

Setting up a watering system in your greenhouse will significantly cut down on the work needed to maintain it. There are three basic rules about watering. First, the planting medium should drain well. A plant cannot be watered well if the medium does not drain properly. Second, watering needs to be thorough every time. The water needs to reach the roots for a healthy plant to grow. Check this by moving the soil aside a few inches deep with your finger. If it is still dry an inch down, the plant needs more water. Third, water before the plant gets stressed out. This often means the soil will be dry but not parched.

An irrigation system can ensure that the plants are getting all the water they need and at the appropriate times.

Hand watering

Simple and self-explanatory, hand watering is holding the hose or can in your hand to apply water to the plants. This is, of course, the most time intensive and inefficient method. It is also the least expensive and easiest to do.

Misting system

A mister sends water droplets over the tops of the plants. The system is attached to the roof of the greenhouse. Misting systems can be set up to deliver water to the plants on a schedule for the highest effectiveness. These are most often used in greenhouses that contain all the same kind of plant and therefore need all the same regime of watering.

Nozzles can become clogged, so the system needs to be checked regularly and maintained consistently. Another downside is that a lot of water is wasted since the mist goes everywhere. Water can pool up on floors and elsewhere.

Drip tubes

Drip tubes are specially made hoses that have many tiny holes in them. The system is set up with a pump and sends small amounts of water out at a time. The system supports multiple tubes which extend out from the main water supply. The tubes can be buried into the soil around the plant or placed on the soil around them. The system can be set up manually, or automatically with timers and motion sensors.

These are better than the misting system because they don't get the plants' leaves wet. Over-wet leaves can encourage mold and disease.

Mat irrigation

Specialty mats are placed under the container holding the plant. The mats are kept constantly moist through a drip line system. Plants wick up water from the mats as needed, creating a self-watering system. There is no worry of over-watering or under-watering with this system.

Chapter 5: Essential Greenhouse Equipment

Thermometer

Temperature is of utmost importance when managing a greenhouse. Thermometers range in cost from simple and inexpensive to ultra-fancy and very expensive. A high/low thermometer will display the highest temperature during the day and lowest at night. This is extremely useful when planning your heating and cooling requirements.

Potting containers

Pots in a variety of sizes will be necessary to grow plants. What size you specifically need will depend on what you are growing. Having specific seed starter flats is extremely helpful for starting any seeds.

Gardening tools

The basics, a trowel, shovel, rake, hand fork, pruners, and a watering can. If there is space, a wheelbarrow will be very useful. Designate an area of your greenhouse for tool storage. It is amazing how quickly things can go missing or get misplaced. A marker and labels are also good to have on hand if you are growing a variety of plants.

Sink or washtub

Having a place to rinse garden tools, wash vegetables, and clean pots is very handy.

Cleaning supplies

Insecticidal spray, disinfectant spray, and bleach are a few good things to have in the greenhouse to keep everything clean and free of pests and disease.

Bench and/or shelves

A staging area to do your gardening work is very helpful. When you are transplanting or starting seeds, you always need space on which to set pots, flats, and soil.

Benches and shelves are also needed to hold the pots. Keeping them on the floor is not a good idea for the plant's health.

Humidity monitor/psychrometer

Since humidity can be so tricky in a greenhouse, having a tool that monitors it is invaluable. There are handheld as well as permanently installed versions.

CHAPTER 6: USING SPACE EFFECTIVELY

The way you set up your greenhouse will depend entirely on what size and type of greenhouse you have. There is no right or wrong way, but here are some tips for making the space work well for you. Greenhouse space is finite, and it is highly recommended that you draw out a plan before you start putting anything in it.

Make space for a walkway or paths between your benches, shelves, raised beds or whatever growing containers you intend to use. You should be able to access every plant in the greenhouse within arm's reach. If plants are out of your reach, it will be extremely difficult to care for them properly. Do not sacrifice paths for more growing space. Having more growing space is great, but if you can't tend to the plants, check them for diseases, see if they are getting watered properly and so forth, it will be wasted.

Always have a plan:

- What plants will you be growing?
- How much space will each plant need?
- When will they be transplanted if that is the intention?
- What resources will each plant need?
- Can certain plants be grouped to conserve resources?

Not having a plan will leave you frustrated and running in circles. Deciding last minute how to deal with plants that grew bigger than anticipated, plants that are ready before you are and the like, takes a lot of the fun out of gardening.

Have some temporary tables on hand for those times when extra space is desperately needed. They can be set up and taken down easily and are relatively inexpensive. A table set up outside the greenhouse to hold extra containers, tools, and soil is very helpful.

Shelves can be set up for staging. This means keeping some plants on the lower shelves while you wait for the ones on the upper shelves to mature. This doesn't work with all plants, so plan accordingly.

Divide your greenhouse into zones if possible. With a very small greenhouse, this may be difficult. Zones will assist you in managing the space more effectively. One area of the greenhouse can be for all the shade-loving plants, and there can be shade cloths arranged over the glazing in that area. This will help you stay organized. It will also help to know where all your plants are, so you don't have to go searching for specific ones in the multitude of plants surrounding you.

Use hooks, hanging baskets, and other wall and ceiling attachments to utilize the vertical space around you. Tools can be hung on hooks. Plants can go in baskets. This can greatly increase the available space in your greenhouse.

Chapter 7: Growing in Your Greenhouse

Once you have chosen your greenhouse, built it, and set it up, it is time for the real fun to begin. Growing plants in a greenhouse environment is different from growing them outside in a garden or inside in a grow room. Some things are similar, however there are a variety of different things to consider.

This section will walk you through the process of growing plants from start to finish, including detailed explanations for growing specific vegetables, fruits, and herbs.

Starting Seeds

A greenhouse is not always an ideal place to start plants from seed. It can get too hot during the day unless there is careful temperature control and lots of ventilation. During cold months, the temperature can be too low for the delicate seeds to germinate.

To start seedlings in a greenhouse, be sure to monitor the temperature and keep in mind that different types of plants like different temperatures. A greenhouse that is set up with a lighting and venting system will be much better for starting seeds than one without.

Alternately, seeds grown in winter will have the opposite problem. During the day, the seeds are warm and happy. Once night falls and the temperature drops, the germination process can be terminated, and the seeds will be lost. The temperature should be at least 50°F at all times, with the optimal temperature being between 65°F-80°F. If you are starting seeds in winter in your greenhouse, you will need an additional heat source. Please see the section about planting in winter for more information about this.

Starting seeds in a greenhouse is a great way to jump-start the growing season and have seedlings ready to plant in the ground as soon as the outside temperature allows. If this is your goal, start your seedlings in the greenhouse 6-8 weeks before the last frost date for your area. If it is too cold at night for the seedlings, you can use heat mats under them. Seedling heat mats can alleviate the issue of low temperatures. They require electricity which means your greenhouse will need access to power to take advantage of this. Starting seeds in a cold frame greenhouse without an additional heat source is not viable until the outside temperatures are amenable.

There are cool weather plants (kale, cabbage, broccoli) and hot weather plants (tomatoes, peppers, eggplant), and if the temperature is an issue, you can choose ones that are better suited for your greenhouse. Read the seed packets to see which ones will work best for your situation.

Planting

Seeds can be planted in open flat seed trays or in individual plug trays. There are several different options on the market that work well. Reusable Styrofoam plug trays are a good choice and come in a variety of plug sizes. The benefit of individual plug trays over flat seed trays is that with the individual ones, the roots of the plants don't intertwine, which can make them difficult to remove. Also, the seedlings can be popped out easily and placed in the garden.

A general all-purpose potting mix will work well. Many people prefer a soil-less mix. Plant the seeds according to the depth indicated on the packet. It varies by seed. Often, seeds are planted too deeply when all they need is a light covering. Planting them too deeply means they will likely not germinate.

The trays should be on tables or benches to germinate.

If your greenhouse has dirt floors and that is the only place you intend to plant seeds, you will have to wait until the soil is warm enough to get started. This will be sooner than if you were planting in the soil outside since the sun is heating the inside soil like a battery.

Watering

In the beginning, seedlings only need a light mist of water. They can drown or rot if they are over-watered, so go easy. Of course, they can also die if they aren't watered enough. A good rule of thumb is to mist them until the soil is moist, and that's it. They need to be watered at least twice a day to prevent them from drying out. A spray bottle is a good way to water newly planted seeds.

When the seeds have germinated, they can be watered deeper, and it is good to allow the soil to dry between watering.

Light

Newly planted seeds need between 14-16 hours of light. Using grow lights may be necessary depending on where you live and what time of year it is. The lights should be adjustable, so you can raise them higher as the plants grow. In the beginning, you want them to be as close to the seedlings as possible without touching them.

Pollination

Plant pollination happens in nature through birds, bees, butterflies, and the wind. A greenhouse, with its controlled environment, is a barrier to all these. This means alternate methods of pollination must happen for your plants to produce fruits. Manual pollination is done by gently shaking or tapping flowers to release the pollen. Different plants have different ways of pollinating. For example, a squash is either male or female. The pollen needs to be transferred from one plant to the other. Each tomato plant has both male and female flowers, so the pollen needs to be disturbed enough so it distributes within itself.

Garden and greenhouse supply companies sell battery operated pollinating devices. They are handheld wands that vibrate the flower head gently. A hand-held electric toothbrush will serve the same purpose. For best results, pollinate plants every day in the morning.

WHAT TO PLANT IN YOUR GREENHOUSE

A greenhouse provides excellent growing conditions for a large number of plants. With a greenhouse setup, you can rotate crops with the seasons. A greenhouse is also an ideal place for successive planting. This means that you plant your next crop while the current one is maturing. The plants are then ready to harvest one after another, and you have a continuous supply of fresh vegetables.

Getting a jump start on the growing season by starting your seeds in the greenhouse is the goal of many gardeners. It is best to start with the plants that take the longest to produce fruit. For example, tomatoes need a long season, so getting them started a few weeks early makes a big difference. Vegetables that don't take long to grow can be planted in a greenhouse, and they will do well. If you have limited space though, then you'll want to reserve it for the plants that need it most.

Plants that do well with an early start include tomatoes, kale, broccoli, cauliflower, collard greens, peas, and arugula. Some types of vegetables do better in a cold frame greenhouse rather than a heated one. These include carrots, lettuces, and cool weather herbs. There are several companies that develop seed varieties specifically for growing in a greenhouse.

Warm season vegetables such as peppers, tomatoes, beans, cucumbers, eggplant and summer squash need a daytime temperature of at least 60°F and a nighttime temperature of at least 55°F.

Cold season vegetables such as beets, cabbage, cauliflower, carrots, turnips, peas, radishes, broccoli, lettuce, and chard need a daytime temperature between 50°F-70°F and a nighttime temperature of at least 45°F.

HOW TO GROW VEGETABLES IN A GREENHOUSE

Peppers

Just about every variety of pepper will grow well in a greenhouse. There are many types to choose from, sweet peppers to hot peppers, and they will all thrive in your greenhouse environment. The temperature at night must be above 55°F for them to grow well. This will require waiting until the temperature outside is high enough to start them or ensuring that you have a heat source you can turn on at night to help them out.

Choose a variety that grows tall instead of growing outwards and becoming bushy. Space is usually at a premium in a greenhouse, and so it is best to choose those that aren't going to take up a lot of room. The plants need to be spaced appropriately, or diseases can bloom.

Peppers are slow to germinate. Getting a head start on the growing season by starting the seedlings in the greenhouse will make a huge difference in how soon they are ready to harvest. Pepper seeds need warm soil and being in the controlled atmosphere of a greenhouse is perfect for them. When the outside temperatures are high enough for planting outside, you will have strong, sturdy seedlings ready to transplant.

Seven to ten weeks before the date you want to move the seedlings to the garden, plant the seeds in the greenhouse. The planned date to move them to the garden should be around two-three weeks after the last expected frost. Transplanting seedlings directly after the last expected frost is too chancy since there is still the possibility of a frost occurring. It is unlikely the pepper plants would make it through a frost. Therefore, giving a few weeks of buffer time is ideal.

All the containers you will be using to plant the seeds should be sterilized. This is to ensure the greenhouse remains a clean environment. It would be awful to transport diseases or pests into the enclosed area of a greenhouse where they can spread quickly. A solution of one part bleach to nine parts water is good. Soak the containers for ten minutes, then rinse in clean water and dry. You can also use apple cider vinegar in place of bleach. If you're using Styrofoam planting plugs, a good washing with a hose or pressure washer is great. Also, they can be soaked in a garbage can and then rinsed. Whichever method you use to clean your containers, make sure they are washed thoroughly afterwards and dried completely as bleach and vinegar can have a detrimental effect on seeds.

Fill the planting containers with a soil-less mix designed for seed starting. These mixes are readily available at garden centers. Water the soil until it is moist and cohesive. Soil-less mixes are difficult to soak at first, so it will likely take a few passes to get it totally wet.

Make a ½" indentation on the top of the soil and place the pepper seed inside. Cover the seeds lightly with soil. Place a layer of clear plastic wrap over the containers to increase the warmth inside.

The soil needs to be between 65°F-95°F to germinate. If your greenhouse is not heated, you'll need to place heat mats underneath the pots to bring the temperature up.

Seedlings will emerge in eight days to three weeks, depending on the warmth of the soil and the type of pepper. Hot pepper varieties take longer to germinate. When the plants start to come up, take off the plastic wrap and move them to an area in the greenhouse that gets a lot of light.

The seedlings will grow better if the daytime temperature is between 65°F-70°F during the day and 60°F-65°F at night. You may need to add heat to your greenhouse to maintain these temperatures. When the seedlings have developed their first set of leaves, thin them if necessary or transplant them to larger pots so they have more room to grow.

Water your pepper plants regularly and fertilize them with a water-soluble mixture once or twice a week. It is helpful for strengthening the plant to let the soil dry out between waterings. The soil should be watered until it is moist but not soaked.

A week before you intend to plant the peppers in the garden (when the soil temperature outdoors is consistently reaching at least 65°F), harden them off. This entails removing them from the greenhouse and setting them outside in a protected place for a couple of hours each day to get them acclimated to the outdoor conditions. Gradually extend the time they are left out. Plant the peppers in your garden in a location that gets full sun.

Lettuce

As long as the temperature is above 45°F, lettuce will do really well in a greenhouse environment. Even an unheated greenhouse will be okay. When the temperature gets hot though, lettuce and other greens don't do well. This is a cool-season crop. Leaf lettuce tolerates heat better than head lettuce.

Lettuce can be planted in containers, or if you have a dirt floor, they can be seeded directly into the soil. They need full sun, so choose a spot in the greenhouse where they will get at least six hours of direct sunlight.

Clean and sterilize planting containers as per the instructions listed in the section about peppers. Fill containers with a good soil-less potting mix and soak with water. The soil-less potting mixes don't absorb water well at first, so it will take a few passes with the hose to get them completely wet. Plant seeds ¼-1/2" deep and 1" apart. The seeds will take 35-45 days to mature and be ready for harvest. The soil should be kept moist but not waterlogged.

The greenhouse should be kept between 50°F and 70°F. Any higher than this and the lettuce will wilt. If it is too warm, open vents and doors to keep the temperature down. The nighttime temperature is best if it is between 45°F and 55°F. A few colder nights won't kill the lettuce, and a few extra hot days won't hurt it either but try to minimize that as much as possible.

Lettuce actually has an interesting survival technique for freezing temperatures. When the temperature drops, the lettuce plants relocate water out of their cells into the intercellular spaces to ensure the freezing temperature doesn't destroy the cell walls. When this happens, their leaves will go limp, and it will look like the entire crop has died off. However, as soon as they are in sunlight and the greenhouse warms up, they re-hydrate and look alive again.

Lettuce can be harvested directly in the greenhouse. It doesn't need to be transplanted outside; however, it can be if desired. To harvest lettuce, cut the leaves off when they are 3-6" tall. Cut them

½" above the stem, and they will regrow again and again. It is possible to harvest four or five times before the plant is spent.

Lettuce can also be grown in the winter. It will take longer to germinate and mature, usually 50-80 days instead of 45 days, yet it is worth it to have freshly grown lettuce in the middle of winter. See the section about winter crop growing for more information.

Peas

A cool weather vegetable, peas do well in a greenhouse. Even in wintertime, they are truly an all-season vegetable when you have a greenhouse. The two main varieties of peas are snow peas and snap peas. Both have the same growing requirements and can thrive in a greenhouse space. Peas are winter crops, but still some places are too cold for them. There are cold-resistant varieties that fare better in places with snow and freezing temperatures.

Clean and sterilize all containers and pots as described in the section on growing peppers. The greenhouse is a clean space, and it would be awful to inadvertently bring in pests or diseases.

A greenhouse can be used to grow peas at almost any time of year. They can be started in a greenhouse in early spring and then transplanted to the garden after the threat of frost has passed. Early autumn, early winter, and late winter are all possibilities as well. The only time peas don't like to grow is in the intense heat of the summer sun. In fall and winter, the peas will grow entirely in the greenhouse. They will take a bit of setting up and a bunch of patience, yet it is entirely worth it for fresh peas. They will take longer to germinate and grow in the depth of cold weather. Usually, peas take 50-55 days to get to maturity. In winter, this is extended to 3-4 months.

To grow peas for a winter garden, start them in late September. Use a rich soil-less potting mix for best results. Fill the containers and then water the potting mix, so it is thoroughly moist. It takes a little while for it to absorb water, and so it may take a few passes. Plant the seeds 1" deep.

The soil should be always moist but don't let it get waterlogged. Set the containers in a place where they can drain well. The soil temperature needs to be at least 40°F for the seeds to germinate. If it is colder than that in your area, using a heating mat under the containers will work well. Several layers of frost blankets placed over the seeds is another option that has worked well for many gardeners in cold locations.

Once the seeds have sprouted, they need a daytime temperature of around 75°F. Since there isn't as much sun in winter, the seedlings may need you to provide them with more heat. It depends on how warm it gets in your greenhouse during the day. A thermometer is a good tool to have in the greenhouse for this reason. If it is particularly cold where you live, leaving several layers of frost blankets over the peas should give them the heat they need.

They need a minimum of six hours of sunlight per day. They will do better if they receive more. If you add grow lamps, they should be adjustable so as the plant grows they can be moved upwards to accommodate this. The light should be placed no more than two feet above the plant.

When the seedlings reach 5" tall, transplant them to larger pots. Put a trellis, at least three feet high, in the pot behind the plant. Carefully wrap the shoots around the trellis and encourage them as they grow, to use the trellis for support. Handle the plant carefully as it has a shallow root system and can be pulled up easily.

Pick the pea pods as they become ready. This will encourage further production, and you can be eating fresh pea pods for quite a while.

HOW TO GROW FRUITS IN A GREENHOUSE

It may be surprising to some that a good variety of fruits can also be grown in a greenhouse. Greenhouses are not just for vegetables. Grapes, peaches, nectarines, plums, figs, and citrus fruits can all thrive in a greenhouse setting. Many don't even need a heated greenhouse. In Europe, greenhouses were called orangeries since they were originally built to grow oranges.

Grapes

Early fruiting, hardy varieties of grapes do best especially if you are in a colder climate. It isn't necessary to have a heated greenhouse. They will do fine in a cold frame.

Grapes spread out a lot, so before planting them, make sure you have enough room in your greenhouse. A single grapevine is enough for a small greenhouse as it will really spread out. If you have a larger greenhouse, multiple grape vines can be planted three feet apart.

Ideally, the greenhouse can be designed specifically for the purpose of growing grapes to create the optimal conditions. There should be 7-8 feet between the two long walls, so the grapes have enough room to grow. A milky colored polycarbonate glazing is best. Clear glazing materials bring in too much harsh, direct, sunlight. The milky colored glazing lets in enough sun without being overwhelming. Because grape vines will grow high up in the greenhouse, they will be especially susceptible to intense heat.

Grapes need a lot of light to grow, and it is important that the vines can soak up as much sun as possible. The vines should be planted northeast to southwest for the best growth. With this row alignment, the vines will get the first rays of sunshine in the morning.

A well-ventilated greenhouse is best for growing grapes. They like warmth and dryness. Too much humidity will encourage fungal diseases and decrease pollination. In the summer and fall, the greenhouse vents should be kept open.

The vines will grow best if the roots are planted outside of the greenhouse. The vine would then be trained to go into the greenhouse through gaps at ground level. Alternately, they can be planted directly into the soil at the inside edge of the greenhouse. Vines do best planted opposite the door and then trained to go up the side of the wall and along the ridge of the roof towards the door.

Alternately, grape vines can also be grown in containers. The pot will need to be at least 12"-15" in depth and diameter. In a small greenhouse, this may be preferable. Vines planted in the ground will grow prolifically and may overwhelm the greenhouse space. They will need to be constantly pruned to keep them under control. Growing in a container limits the root growth and thus the size of the plant. The other benefit to growing in pots is that they can be moved outside during the cold months. They are hardy and will do fine outside. In late winter or early spring, the pots can be relocated back inside the greenhouse to give the grapes a head start in their fruiting.

Plant the grape vines at the same depth that they are in the pot to lessen their shock. Before planting, add compost or fertilizer to the hole. A good time to plant grapevines is November and December. The vines can be pruned at this time of year without the stress of bleeding. Bleeding is when a tree or vine leaks sap. It can be light or heavy and is often harmless, but messy. Sometimes it is fatal to the vine though.

In the spring, when the foliage starts to grow, apply a fertilizer every three weeks. High potassium fertilizer, like that used for tomatoes is good. Once the leaves are full, increase the fertilizer applications to weekly. Stop the fertilizer when the grapes begin to ripen so as not to negatively affect their flavor.

Every week during the growing season, the vine should be watered. If the vine is planted outside, the weather may help you out with watering. If the vine is inside the greenhouse, you will need to be attentive to the watering schedule.

Pollination occurs via the wind, so when it comes time to pollinate, open vents and doors to create a cross-breeze that will allow the wind to flow through. Temperature activated windows are great in this situation. Manual pollination in combination with the wind is ideal. With the greenhouse vents open, gently shake the vines or cup your hand and brush it over flowers to transfer pollen between the flowers.

Grapes will need to be trellised. Long, sturdy wooden dowels placed across the rafters are an easy solution. Make sure they are strong since grape vines can get quite heavy. Also, pay attention to their height to ensure you won't be running into the vines every time you walk into the greenhouse.

A grapevine will send out tendrils in all directions in an effort to support itself against any structure it encounters. Remove them as you see them since they will tangle up with the fruits and also allow the vine to go wherever it pleases. Train the vine to go where you want, so it doesn't overwhelm the greenhouse.

Lemons (and other citrus fruits)

Lemons are a great choice for greenhouse growing since they require little attention once they are established. Dwarf lemon trees are best for the size of a greenhouse. There are several varieties to choose from, and they produce the same size fruit as larger trees. With the right temperature and climate, a lemon tree can produce fruit all year round.

Citrus trees need lots of warmth which means that if you live in a cold climate, the greenhouse will need to be heated. This will be especially true at night when temperatures really drop. A minimum nighttime temperature of 50°F is required. The trees won't grow fast, but they will still grow at this temperature. A higher temperature is even better; however, you'll have to determine if the cost of heating is worth it.

Planting the trees in pots is necessary to keep their growth limited. A 10-gallon container is good. Some trees can get quite big and if allowed, will take up your whole greenhouse. A dwarf lemon tree in a pot will grow to between three and five feet. Having them in pots also lets you move them outside during the warm months and then into the protection of the greenhouse once the weather starts to get too cold for them.

A lemon tree likes lots of sun so place the pot near the southern end of your greenhouse. To prevent leaf scalding, set it 1'-2' away from the wall glazing. Water the tree whenever the soil feels dry. The pot should be propped up on bricks or stones, so that water can drain out of the bottom. During the winter, watering can decrease to about once a week. A good rule of thumb is to water whenever the leaves look wilted. When the tree is outside, it may need watering every day. Every month, the tree should be fertilized. In the fall, stop fertilizing, so the tree can rest.

Having a thermometer set near your lemon tree will be very useful to maintain the required temperatures. If the temperature falls below 50°F, turn on the heat. If it goes above 95°F, open the ventilation. During the summer months, if you are keeping your lemon tree in the greenhouse, drape a shade cloth along the southern wall of the greenhouse to prevent the tree from getting too much sun.

Citrus trees do not fare well in frost and often die off if exposed to it for too long. They will be okay in a cold, dark location and will become dormant. They can be kept in a cold greenhouse for protection; however, they will not produce fruit in those conditions. They should be surrounded by a light blocking material or kept in a dark corner. Any amount of light tells the tree that it should be growing and producing fruit, and it won't become dormant. A cold greenhouse is not capable of giving the tree all it needs to produce fruit under these conditions. The tree will get confused and drop its leaves and possibly die. Leaf drop happens when the root temperatures get low at the same time as the leaves are receiving light. The plant tries to grow and can't because the roots are cold, and so it drops its leaves.

To keep the tree in the greenhouse and producing fruit during the winter, it needs to receive light and heat.

The trees can be moved outside when the nighttime temperature is above 55F. Put them in a shady spot first so as not to shock them. Too much sun too fast will sunburn them. Move the trees carefully, because in the spring they will have flowers and small fruit that can be knocked off. In the fall, the trees may be full of fruit and too much jostling of the plant could make the fruit fall off.

Pruning is best done in the winter when the tree is partially dormant. Pay attention to spotted or pale leaves which can indicate a thrip infection which is common in lemon trees.

Peaches (and nectarines)

Peaches and nectarines are similar in structure, and the growing requirements for them are basically the same. They won't produce fruit year-round because the tree needs to go dormant and rest. A greenhouse provides a haven for peach and nectarine trees in the winter. The greenhouse should remain unheated, so the tree can go dormant without the worry of frost hurting it.

Choose the soil carefully when planting. Peach trees strongly dislike heavy wet soil. They want well-drained, light soil that can retain moisture without getting bogged down. Neutral and slightly acid soils are best. The pH should not be below 6.5. If it does go that low, treat the base of the tree with lime in the fall. If the acid is too low, the peach pit will not harden, and the center of the fruit will decay.

Plant peaches and nectarines in large pots that can be moved. In the spring, as with lemon trees, they can be moved outside to take advantage of the warmer outside weather. In the late fall, they should be moved back into the greenhouse for protection. Another option is to leave the tree outside all winter and only move it into the greenhouse for a few weeks in early spring to protect the new buds from frost. This will give you a jump start on the season, and you will have fresh peaches sooner.

HOW TO GROW HERBS IN A GREENHOUSE

There are a lot of herbs that will grow well in a greenhouse environment. A greenhouse can protect the herb plants from the intensity of the summer sun. Greenhouses are also a great way to extend the season for growing herbs, so they can grow earlier and later. Chives, cilantro, dill, parsley, basil, lavender, sage, oregano, and chamomile are good choices for greenhouse growing.

Basil

Basil is simple to grow and does very well in a controlled greenhouse environment. The greenhouse can be used to grow the crop from start to finish or as a place to get a jump start on the season before the seedlings can be transplanted outside.

Clean and sterilize any containers as described in the section on peppers. Fill growing containers or seed starting cubes with a good soil-less potting mix. Water the potting mix thoroughly before planting the seeds. Make a ½" indentation in the potting soil and place the seeds in. Cover them lightly with the potting mix. If you have a greenhouse with a dirt floor, basil can be planted directly in the ground.

To germinate, basil seeds need to be around 70°F. If your greenhouse is not heated, the containers will need to be placed on heating pads. Covering the top with a layer of clear plastic wrap will help keep the temperature up until they germinate. Once the seedlings start to show, remove the plastic wrap. If the seedlings are in starter plugs, they should be transplanted to 4" pots.

Basil seedlings are prone to damping off which is a fungal disease caused by the roots being over-watered and remaining damp for too long. After they've grown a bit, water the basil plants once a week, letting the soil dry out between watering. Over-watering will cause the bottom leaves to turn yellow.

Ideally, basil needs six-eight hours of full sun per day to thrive. Depending on your greenhouse setup, you may need to add additional heat and lighting during cool seasons with less sun.

On hot summer days, make use of the greenhouse ventilation. Basil can easily die from overheating.

If the seedlings are being transplanted to your garden, harden them off beforehand. Set them outside for a couple of hours one day and then slowly increase the time they spend outside. Taking them straight from a heated greenhouse to the garden will shock them, and the plants will suffer and may not survive.

When the plants are 6-8" tall, they are ready to be harvested. Harvest basil by pinching off the leaves. The plant will continue to grow and produce for quite a while if you continuously harvest it.

Parsley

Like basil, parsley can be planted in pots, raised beds, or directly into the ground if you have a dirt floor in your greenhouse.

Parsley is very slow to germinate and can take up to a month. To speed up the process, soak the seeds in very warm water (110°F) overnight before planting. Remove any seeds that float. Plant the seeds immediately and be sure to keep the soil moist until the seeds sprout.

Follow the process listed in the section on peppers to clean and sterilize any pots you will be using before bringing them into the greenhouse. Use a high-quality soil-less potting mix to plant the seeds. They should be planted ¼-1/2" in the soil. A good method for doing this is by pressing the seed into the soil to the correct depth. This is easier than making tiny holes to plant each seed into. Cover the tray or pots with plastic wrap to keep the soil warm and moist. Once the seeds sprout, remove the plastic wrap.

Parsley seeds do not fare well in cool temperatures. If you are cultivating them to be transplanted into your garden, plant them just two-three weeks before the last expected frost in your area. A cold frame greenhouse may need heating pads underneath the pots to keep the seedlings warm. The optimal growing temperature for parsley is between 65°-75°F. A heated greenhouse or the use of heating mats is especially beneficial for parsley seedlings.

Set the pots up in a way that they can drain easily. Parsley likes to be well watered, yet it isn't good to flood them.

Once parsley has sprouted, it likes cool temperatures. Partially shaded areas are preferred. In a greenhouse when there are long days of sun, a shade cloth set-up would be nice for the parsley plants.

Before transplanting the seedlings into your garden, harden them off a week beforehand. Set them outside for an hour or two at a time, increasing the amount of time as you go. This helps the seedlings acclimate to the outdoor temperature and climate.

Parsley will be ready to harvest ten-twelve weeks after being planted. Snip the leafy stems off at the base to harvest. The leaves will grow many more times.

CHAPTER 8: SCHEDULING PLANTS FOR YEAR-ROUND GROWING

Plants can be grown year-round in a greenhouse. Proper scheduling with attention to the type of plants, their germination timelines, and the seasons in your area will have you enjoying fresh produce all year. It is highly recommended that you write up a plan before you start planting. This will help determine exactly when to plant and ensure your greenhouse remains organized and productive and that you have the space needed to plant everything you want to. The schedule you come up with will greatly depend on the climate in your area. If you live in a mild region, the greenhouse may not even need to be heated to enjoy all year production. In cold regions, heating the greenhouse may be a prohibitive cost. The only way to know for sure what works in your greenhouse and in your region is to experiment. Try growing a variety of plants using different heating methods and see how it goes.

For many gardeners, growing crops in winter requires providing extra heat for them using one of the methods described in the section on heat sources. Alternately, you can choose particular vegetables and specific varieties of vegetables that will tolerate colder conditions. The greenhouse is a good home in the winter for many vegetables; it keeps temperature extremes at bay and protects the plants from snow, wind, and rain.

Lettuce is a good crop to grow. Herbs, root vegetables like potatoes and carrots, peas, onions, and garlic are also good vegetables to grow in winter.

The biggest problem with winter growing is the shorter days which mean smaller amounts of sunlight. Temperature is also an issue; however, it is the lack of light that will likely hurt the plants the most. To get around this, it is important to plan your growing season, so that the plants have completed most of their growth before the shortest days occur. The plants will survive the cold yet will remain sad and dormant while they wait for sunnier days.

The upside to growing in the winter, besides having fresh vegetables year-round, is that the plants don't die as quickly. In the middle of summer, if you let your ripe vegetables sit too long in the elements, they will spoil. With winter greenhouse gardening, a ripe head of lettuce will stay fresh and in good condition inside the greenhouse for months.

Hardy vegetables, ones that are frost-tolerant, can be planted in December and January. These include beets, leafy greens, spinach, turnips, radishes, and carrots. They take seven-twelve weeks to germinate so be patient. In February and March, these plants can be hardened off and transplanted to your garden. In places where there is snow, you may need to wait until April. Beets and carrots can be started and transplanted all the way through September.

Spinach is a great cold-hardy winter vegetable. It grows quickly, so you can do several plantings of it and have fresh spinach all winter long. Other greens, such as kale, mustard, chard, raab, and a variety of oriental greens are also great choices.

There are varieties of lettuce that are frost resistant. Some more than others. So, even though it is usually planted with the cool-season plants, some types can be planted earlier. Experiment to see which ones work best in your greenhouse. Plant a lot of different varieties. This is also nice because it will give you a variety in your salads for the winter months that is very enjoyable.

As the hardy vegetables are maturing and waiting to be transplanted, start the cool-season plants. Broccoli, cabbage, cauliflower, and lettuce can be started in March. These vegetables need growing temperatures between 55°-65°F, so if your greenhouse is colder than that, you will have to add heating pads or layers of frost covers. They also take between seven-twelve weeks to germinate. Once the outside temperature is amenable to transplanting these varieties, harden them off and put them in the garden.

In March and April, warm season vegetables can be started. If you are in a cold zone, the plants will absolutely need additional heat. They will not tolerate frost. Alternately, you can wait until mid-April or May to start them. Tomatoes, beans, eggplant, peas, corn, melons, squash, and peppers take four-eight weeks to germinate. Once the average outside temperature reaches 65°-70°F, harden these seedlings off and transplant into the garden.

In temperate regions, a second crop of cool-season vegetables can be started in July and August. Hardy vegetables can be planted in the garden in late fall and over winter, ready for a spring harvest.

CHAPTER 9: HYDROPONICS IN A GREENHOUSE

Turning a greenhouse into a hydroponics growing space can be done quite easily. And, without costing a fortune either. It will take a little adjustment in space and growing techniques, but it is not difficult.

Greenhouse growing is all about controlling the environment around you to create the best possible situation so plants can thrive. Hydroponics has that same goal. Combining the two creates the best of both worlds and makes an amazing space for plants to grow quickly and vigorously.

Basically, the greenhouse can become the dedicated space for growing hydroponically. All six hydroponic systems can be set up in a greenhouse. There will need to be some rearranging and re-purposing of space, but other than that, it won't take much. Hydroponics requires lighting and heating methods just like greenhouse gardening. The humidity and climate need to be controlled carefully to protect the plants in both situations.

The cost of growing hydroponically in the greenhouse is less than growing with soil. The soil needed to grow vegetables adds up fast when you're planting large quantities. Hydroponics eliminates that cost entirely. A hydroponic garden that is not in a greenhouse must use a lot of electricity to make sure there is adequate light and heat for the plants. A greenhouse provides a lot of heat and light naturally from the sun which makes the cost of growing hydroponically less expensive too. Like regular greenhouse gardening, the only time you will need to supplement heat or light is during cool months with shorter days.

A greenhouse will need access to electricity and have an external heat source (other than the sun) to be conducive for hydroponic growing. A tunnel greenhouse or hoop house won't work; however, an A-frame, dome, post, and rafter or attached greenhouse would make a great location for hydroponics.

Plants that do well in a hydroponic greenhouse are tomatoes (they thrive!), lettuce, mint, basil, cabbage, strawberries, and green beans. Plants that take up a lot of room, like pumpkins or any melon, will not work well in a greenhouse with its limited space.

A hydroponic greenhouse can not only extend your growing season, but it can increase your productivity. Plants growing in soil take longer to mature. Greenhouse hydroponic plants will grow fast because the conditions are perfect for them, and they will be abundant because the environment is set-up for their success.

CHAPTER 10: MANAGING AND OPERATING A GREENHOUSE

The health and productivity of your greenhouse depends on thorough and efficient management. Creating optimal growing conditions for a variety of plants with a wide variance of needs can get complicated. It isn't difficult, yet without planning, it can be chaotic. Chaos breeds mistakes and it is the plants you are trying to grow that will suffer. Plants can get forgotten or be placed into climate situations which aren't good for them if there isn't the appropriate planning.

Creating and keeping a schedule of what you are growing, and the individual needs and growth schedules of each crop will make your greenhouse run smoothly and keep your plants happy and healthy.

CLEANING A GREENHOUSE/PREPARING FOR THE NEXT SEASON

Greenhouses can become dirty places. After all, you are dealing with actual dirt. It's not just the inside that needs to be cleaned though. Glass windows need to be cleaned. If there are gutters, they will need to be cleaned out. Set aside at least one day a year to give the greenhouse a thorough cleaning. For greenhouses that are used only as season-extenders, clean them in the late fall after the growing season is done. For those that are used all year round, clean in the fall when there are mild temperatures. For periodically used greenhouses, clean them in-between uses.

A clean greenhouse is necessary for the health of the plants. Diseases can grow in dirty conditions. Pests can prosper. Dirty glazing will hinder the amount of light that comes in.

To clean a greenhouse:

1. Remove all the plants to a protected area.

2. Take a broom or vacuum and remove all the debris from the floor.

3. Wash down all the structural parts of the greenhouse. Use a disinfectant or detergent that is not harmful to plants. There are specialty greenhouse cleaning solutions available.

4. Wash the inside and outside of the glazing materials. If it is plastic, test a small piece first to make sure you won't damage it. If you used shade paint, wash that off too.

5. Scrape out dirt between panes. A flexible plastic plant label works great for this.

6. Replace or fix anything that is broken.

7. Clean out the gutters if you have them.

Greenhouses are fragile in places so exercise caution, especially when cleaning the glazing and anyplace higher than your reach. Do not lean against walls. There are long handheld tools available to reach high places. Wear gloves and safety glasses if you are dealing with glass.

Before you start growing the next round of crops in your greenhouse, make sure all the systems are in working order. Assess all the vents to ensure they are opening and closing properly. Inspect the frame and glazing for cracks, chips, breaks, or anything else that will need to be repaired before you house plants in there again. Inspect your shade covers and purchase more if needed. Take inventory of your pots and tools to make sure there are enough and are the ones that you need. If you have a watering system, check it over for leaks or blockages. If there is a heating or cooling system, inspect it to make sure it will continue operating correctly. Take inventory of your insecticides, cleaning materials, soil, and other growing mediums to ensure there is enough.

Take a moment and evaluate the previous growing season. Is there anything you wished you had had at that time? Additional vents? Bigger pots? A different tool? Paver stones to walk on instead of gravel? Every year of greenhouse gardening is a year to learn new things. Take these lessons and apply them to the next year. Make the greenhouse work for you.

CHAPTER 11: PESTS & DISEASES

Cleanliness is the best way to prevent pests. Make sure any new plants that are brought into the greenhouse are pest and disease free. If any of them carries anything, it can quickly spread through the enclosed space of the greenhouse. If you see any plants with pests or disease, immediately remove them from the greenhouse. A good plan is to place any new plant outside the greenhouse for a few days as quarantine before bringing it inside.

Mesh should be placed over all ventilation openings to reduce the chance of pests entering the greenhouse. Any crack or holes that appear in the walls should be attended to immediately.

Greenhouses are great because they do eliminate a lot of potential pests and infestations that occur outside. However, that is a double-edged sword because often outside there are predators that eat and help fend off pests. When the balance of nature is changed, these predators are no longer there to help us, and so we need to tackle the problems differently.

The majority of insects and pests reproduce at a fast rate, and a small infestation can quickly become a huge one. Check your plants frequently. Pay close attention to any signs of distress. Look under leaves and on stems.

The type of pest or disease that shows up in your greenhouse will depend on your location and what you are growing; however, there are a few common ones to watch out for.

THRIPS

These tiny little pests require a multifaceted treatment approach. They are usually a yellowish-green color but can also be other colors. The larvae leave a shiny trail and teeny black specks of fecal matter on leaf surfaces. Blue sticky traps will combat the adults who fly around. An insecticide for soft-bodied insects will take care of the larvae and eggs on the plant.

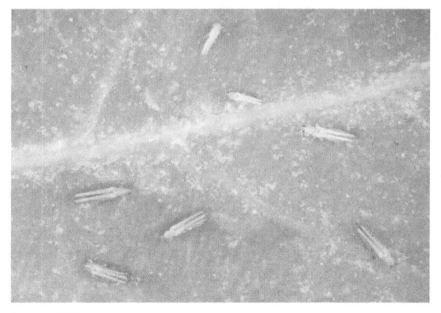

Protasov AN/Shutterstock.com

APHIDS

These little tear-shaped bugs are found on the undersides of leaves. They can be green, brown, black, yellow and pink. Signs of an aphid infestation include wilting and generally unhealthy-looking plants. An insecticide specifically for soft-bodied insects works well to get rid of them.

WHITEFLIES

These look like little white moths and will fly around when the foliage is disturbed, making them easy to identify. In small numbers, they aren't harmful to the plants, but if left on their own, they will multiply and become a problem. They leave a shiny residue on leaves that will turn into black mold if it builds up too much. Sticky traps are good for catching the adults. An insecticide for soft-bodied insects will take care of the eggs and larvae.

D. Kucharski K. Kucharska/Shutterstock.com

MEALYBUGS

These bugs create easily identifiable cotton ball-like masses in the joints of plants. They drink the sap of leaves and stems causing plants to wilt and leaves to turn yellow. An insecticide for soft-bodied insects will take care of them. Continue treatment even after it looks like they are gone. They often reappear weeks or months later.

SPIDER MITES

If you see little yellow specks all over your plants, you have a spider mite infestation. There may also be webbing between the branches and leaves. A miticide is needed to get rid of these pests. Treat the plants for at least a month because spider mite eggs are notoriously hard to destroy, and they will hatch even after being sprayed.

ZenkyPhoto/Shutterstock.com

FUNGUS

Overly wet conditions can cause a variety of fungal diseases such as powdery mildew, botrytis, root rot, and phytophthora. All plants should have good drainage to prevent these diseases. Signs of a fungal infection are wilted plants, yellowing, collapse, or development of fuzzy growths on the leaves and stems. Fungal diseases can be treated with neem oil. Some plants can't be treated with neem oil so do your research before using it.

BACTERIAL DISEASE

These diseases are incurable. Signs include plant tissue looking like it is melting and turning into a sticky mess and water-soaked spots. Any plants showing these signs need to be immediately removed from the greenhouse and destroyed. Bacterial diseases are spread through dirty containers, tools, and clothing. A clean greenhouse with plenty of air circulation is the key to preventing these diseases.

VIRUSES

There are many types of viruses. The most common symptom is yellow rings or a mosaic pattern on leaves. Viruses are usually brought in by insects and pests, which is another reason to treat any pest infestations immediately and thoroughly. Viruses are not treatable, and any plants showing signs need to be removed from the greenhouse and destroyed.

GETTING STARTED

Having a greenhouse can be very rewarding. It is a useful tool and can enhance any garden. The possibilities that a greenhouse can provide are numerous. From a small, portable, fold-up, greenhouse to a large, heated, permanent one, the potential for greater garden production is endless. If you're not sure how much you will use a greenhouse, start with a small, non-permanent one and see how you like it. There is always a learning curve with new things, so don't be disheartened if it doesn't go perfectly. Every greenhouse situation is different, and even master gardeners can run into unexpected problems. So keep experimenting and most importantly have fun with your greenhouse!

Appendix: Temperature and Light Requirements for Your Plant

Plant	Heat (Min|Max)	Heat (optimum)	Light (minimum)
Beans	45°F|80°F	75°F	4-6 hours
Beets	32°F|85°F	70°F	4-6 hours
Carrots	32°F|85°F	70°F	4-8 hours
Celery	45°F|70°F	65°F	4-6 hours
Chard	32°F|90°F	70°F	6 hours
Corn	55°F|100°F	85°F	6-8 hours
Cucumber	60°F|95°F	80°F	6-8 hours
Eggplant	60°F|95°F	75°F	4-6 hours
Lettuce	28°F|80°F	60°F-70°F	3-4 hours
Melons	60°F|95°F	85°F	8 hours
Onions	55°F|85°F	65°F	6 hours
Peas	32°F|80°F	70°F	4-6 hours
Peppers	60°F|90°F	75°F	4-8 hours
Potatoes	45°F|80°F	70°F	6-8 hours
Radishes	40°F|85°F	70°F	6 hours
Spinach	28°F|75°F	65°F	3-4 hours
Squash	60°F|90°F	80°F	8 hours
Strawberries	60°F|80°F	75°F	6 hours
Tomatoes	60°F-62°F|95°F	75°F	8 hours
Cabbage family (Broccoli, Cabbage, Cauliflower, Brussels Sprouts, Kohlrabi, Kale)	28°F|75°F		4-6 hours

Review Page

First of all, thank you for purchasing this book. I know you could have picked any number of books to read, but you picked this book and for that I am extremely grateful.

If you enjoyed this book and found some benefit in reading this, I'd like to hear from you and hope that you could take some time to post a review on Amazon.

I wish you all the best for your gardening journey!

ABOUT THE AUTHOR

Richard's father was a keen gardener and that is where his interest in all natural things began. As a youngster, he enjoyed nothing better than helping his father in the garden.

Nowadays, he finds himself at the opposite end of life. Having had a satisfying career, he now has time to potter around in his garden and take care of his small homestead. Much of the food on his dinner table is homegrown. He likes to experiment with various gardening methods and find new ways to grow bountiful crops year-round.

He wants to share his knowledge and show how easy and rewarding it is to set up your own prosperous garden. In his opinion, you don't need a huge budget to get started. When you do get started, you will soon feel, and taste, the benefits of growing your own food.

Learn more about Richard Bray at amazon.com/author/richardbray

Made in the USA
Monee, IL
29 October 2024